TWENTY

# TWENTY

## south carolina poetry fellows

▲▲▼▲▲

*edited by Kwame Dawes*

HUB CITY writing project

2005

First printing, January 2005

Cover artwork, *Let's Play*, by Marcelo Novo 1994, acrylic on canvas, 20"x16"
    from the private collection of Karen Watson and Charlie Holmes
Cover and book design—Mark Olencki
Page editors & proofreaders—Pamela Ivey Huggins, Betsy Wakefield Teter,
    and Jill McBurney
Printed by McNaughton & Gunn, Inc., Michigan

Library of Congress Cataloging-in-Publication Data

Twenty : South Carolina poetry fellows / edited by Kwame Dawes.
    p. cm.
  ISBN 1-891885-39-1 (alk. paper)
  1. American poetry—South Carolina. 2. South Carolina—Poetry. 3.
Poetry—Authorship. I. Title: 20. II. Dawes, Kwame Senu Neville, 1962- III.
Hub City Writers Project.
  PS558.S6T89 2005
  811'.60809757—dc22
                        2004022171

Hub City Writers Project
Post Office Box 8421
Spartanburg, South Carolina 29305
(864) 577-9349 • fax (864) 577-0188 • www.hubcity.org

# Poetry Fellows

# Preface

*Twenty*, a collaboration between the South Carolina Arts Commission and the Hub City Writers Project, is a collection of poetry by winners of the South Carolina Arts Commission's Poetry Fellowships, celebrating more than two decades of this annual program. The Commission's Artist Fellowships (www.southcarolinaarts.com) recognize and reward the artistic achievements of South Carolina's exceptional individual artists in a variety of arts disciplines.

Since 1977, the Poetry Fellowships have recognized new and established poets, and this fine collection demonstrates the range and excellence of the Fellows' work.

Distinguished judges for the fellowship awards have included Jayne Cortez, Inez Collette, Robert Creeley, Toi Derricotte, Gary Soto, Joseph Torra, David Trinidad, and Ellen Bryant Voigt.

We extend thanks to the many, many poets who participated in the Fellowship Program over the years, and especially to those published here whose art and talent made this collection possible. Thanks also to our superb organizational partner, the Hub City Writers Project.

Deepest appreciation to Kwame Dawes, professor and distinguished poet-in-residence at the University of South Carolina, whose introduction guides and inspires us. A gifted poet himself, Kwame is director and founder of The South Carolina Poetry Initiative (www.cla.sc.edu/engl/poetry/).

Special thanks to Gwen Boykin, Joyce Bibby, and Clay Burnette of the South Carolina Arts Commission, and to the South Carolina State Library and its director, Jim Johnson, who made sure this book will be on the shelves in every public library in the state.

It has been a privilege to be part of the collaborative and creative process that led to the publication of *Twenty*. Readers who are already devoted to poetry and readers new to poetry will take great pleasure in this volume.

—Sara June Goldstein
Director of Literary Arts
South Carolina Arts Commission

# Introduction
## by Kwame Dawes

There is some value in the suggestion that we should pay as little attention to a poet's pontifications about his or her art as we can. The idea, of course, is that the poet has only the semblance of authority about his or her work, but is really only able to speak of what he or she is trying to do from the position of one limited witness of the verse. The idea is a romantic one—one that suggests that the poem is essentially the property of the world and that it is open to all interpretations and meanings. The poet, then, has to relinquish all connection to the poem once the poem is published, spoken, or shared with others in some way. The problem with this idea is that it is supported most doggedly by people who discovered this idea as a wonderful "out" for them when they could not understand a poet while in grade school. The cult of opinion is now an American birthright ("It's my opinion, so by dint of this, it is a valid and correct view even if it runs against all logic, wisdom, and knowledge—true democracy").

Lovers of poetry are not genuine about their faith in this idea of open interpretation. This may be because of a certain insecurity—a suspicion that the poet had something quite specific in mind. Very often, they find, they are correct in this assumption. Consequently, they like to read what poets say about the making of poems; they enjoy entry into the secret freemasonry of the poetic art, and they have come to trust that these poets had some clear intention in the making of their poems—insight that could enhance our understanding of the poem.

This is probably why the editors at Hub City decided to ask the poets who made this anthology (because of their selection for the prestigious annual fellowship for poetry granted by the South Carolina

Arts Commission) to not only select the poems they would want represented in the collection, but also to write a brief introduction about the poems and about their own art.

In many ways, this approach could render the function of editor redundant. The same is true about the function of this introduction I am writing. But my interest here is to pull together some ideas and themes that these poets introduce in their work and place them in the context of what I understand to be happening in the poetry scene today. I believe strongly in paying attention to what the poets say about their art. But I believe as strongly in reading the work and trying to see how these things—their prose statements about the art, and the art itself and how we, the readers, encounter it—engage with each other.

There is much that is obvious about the poets collected here. They represent the hope of poetry in America simply because they are poets who are writing, despite the arid landscape, despite being accused of lacking relevance and in a world in which the National Endowment for the Arts is panicked at the decreasing interest in reading creative writing in our society. Of course, they probably survive and thrive because they have never had populist hopes for poetry—they have never been allowed to. Many poets come to poetry in secret. There are few celebrations of poetry successes. I have not heard from anyone in these parts going to a poetry-coming-of-age celebration. There are no public rites of passage for poets. Few poets feel confident about announcing that they are poets. They do so with the natural (albeit somewhat apologetic) sense of faith and defiance that religious people have when they talk about their faith in a world in which faith is allowable as long as it is not foisted on others. "I write poetry because I believe in poetry. You may not, and that is fine, but I do, and I must stay with it." These are all poets who write despite their awareness that they cannot now and may never make a living from writing poetry. Of course it is impractical in a world in which the practical is inextricably linked to material things—making money, having influence, fixing problems, building bridges, buying houses, trading stocks—real things.

A poet understands at once that there is no useful way to say, "I am a poet," except as a tenet of faith—a kind of defiance of the status quo. After all, when the question is asked, "Why?" most poets will say, "I have always wanted to write, I like words, I ..." I have met poets who have even developed a wonderful rhetoric of justification. They declare the value of poetry in the language of motivational speakers. "I want people to hear my story because I have been through a great deal and maybe this will help them deal with the same situation." There is truth to this, but it is a way for us to say that we are as valuable as Oprah, or maybe a good social worker, a minister, a therapist. And many poets, like Columbia poet Cassie Premo Steele, have decided to go into the field of poetry as therapy. We have been able to prove that poetry can help with healing, that poetry can help with self estecm, that poetry can help to secure grants, that poetry is good for PR, that poetry makes the child's brain stronger, that poetry will help children do math, and that poetry will make great politicians of us all. We have to do this. We have to act like preachers, priests, ministers who have to show the relevance of faith to human life when saying, "You will go to hell if you do not believe," does not seem practical enough.

But we all know that at some level, we are compromising, we are somehow trying to justify what we do in terms that the Philistines who detest poetry might understand. The toughest thing for the poet to say is that we write poetry because the emotional life of the human being—that part that connects to something ephemeral, something one can't quite put a price on—that thing in all of us is important and poetry reaches that part and finds its meaning there. You see, poets are reticent about what we do, not because we don't believe in what we do, but because we suspect that the world will not believe in what we do. But there are other good reasons for reticence.

Look at all the poets represented here in this revealing and engaging anthology. None of them dare to say that they write poetry for a living. None are able to say, apparently, that their primary occupation is writing poetry. I am certain that if I met any of them on a bus or in the mall, and I asked what he or she did for a living, none would say at once, "I am a poet." Even novelists happily make such announcements. After all, most aspiring novelists that I know regard the clearest evidence of their success as writers to be their ability to say, like V. S. Naipaul, that having attempted a few odd jobs, I have for fifty years made my living entirely as a writer, entirely, then, as a novelist.

These poets have introduced themselves to us and all of them provide us with remarkable insights into why poets write. Their short essays are wonderful apologies for the art of making poems. Kathleen Whitten, whose occupation as a clinical psychologist has suffered its own share of attacks as a not-too-exact science, is still susceptible to the rhetoric of apology and justification when she talks about poetry—about why she writes:

> But at the end of the day, when I close the books and files
> and turn off the computers, I return home to the glorious
> riot of the inexplicable, my true spiritual home. To the land
> of poetry, a crystal city where everything is clear, even if
> it cannot be fully explained. Where language is its own
> reward—and where the lyric poem gives the best possible

explanation for the contradictory and absurd condition of the world. A science of linear quantitative methods cannot hold them, but poems can. That's why I write poems.

For her, poetry is useful for its failure to be useful and its attendant success in letting us know that everything else is fundamentally useless. Starkey Flythe says almost exactly that in his defiantly surrealistic introduction to his poems: "Poetry perhaps more than other art forms, reveals how little changes in the world." His is a theory that resists the hubris of progress, the very foundation of Western civilization and American optimism. For Flythe, poetry is engaged in image and meter, and those preoccupations will never change. His remains a tenet of faith—a kind of self-justification— after all, if the poet contains all that is permanent, he or she comes as close to deity as anyone can.

Terri McCord roots her own poetic sensibility in relativism—but the idea is the same: poetry will not answer questions, it will ask them. Poetry is useful for its uselessness: "My poetry has a predilection for transformation. Believing that any action or *any*thing is open to interpretation, I strive for a certain ambiguity in language that I hope works on a concrete level, as well as a figurative one that sparks questions as a result."

Like Kathleen Whitten, virtually all the poets in the collection are committed to the poem as a lyric form, as a form of profound personal value. Jan Bailey is most explicit about this. Her poems must satisfy her first. In many ways, her poems seem to exist outside of her—a force that brings her to a place of honesty even beyond herself:

> Occasionally folks are embarrassed by my poems, but I don't mind taking risks if the emotion is honest. I don't mind writing about a swing from sadness, or the longing to be engulfed, or the confusion children feel, probably much more than we know. And this is exactly why I love poetry— because it is always new, experience reinterpreted, language honed and precise, because it gets at what is real and so forgivably human.

Needless to say, she is describing her ideal concept of the poem. And she is describing what poems do for her—what, perhaps, *her* poems do for her. We do feel some relief to know that Bailey is startled by her own honesty—so that when she writes in such a sensual manner about the relationship between a mother and a child in her poem "Encounter," we understand that it is the poem searching for honesty by taking risks. Still, the instinct is fundamentally lyrical—a quest for meaning through personal narrative.

Yet even when poets appear to be grand old iconoclasts, raging against post-modernist disconnect, they remain, at their core, lyrical poets whose confessional addictions are hard to deny. The late S. Paul Rice hectors valiantly against his list of the enemies of the true poetic soul in his essay: "I, as a Southern white man, have assiduously tried to avoid all the straits and arrows created to civilize me and make me respectable: the one-size-fits-all poetic of the Master of Fine Arts degree, the marginalizing of our poet laureate, James Dickey, one of the finest bards to ever ring the 'iron of English'; the painfully earnest chronicle of the confessional poets and their hangers-on. The story of Postmodern poetry is a narrative of disconnection and trivialization, and I disavowed it long ago." Rice ends his essay with a rousing anthem to the lyric spirit complete with its ubiquitous "I": "I place my poetry in the middle of this. I want to wake up in the dark and light the stove. I want to eat rattlesnake muscle for supper. I want to grab the fallen power line, even if it kills me."

It is no accident that Rice's high priest of poetry is James Dickey, for in Dickey we find one quality that overrides all his other complexities: his absolute commitment to the idea of the poet as the true artist, the true bearer of truth and wisdom—as the figure that sits at the top of the pyramid of civilization. Dickey's hubris is as legendary as it is intoxicating and tempting for the poet. He made poets feel good about being poets. He did that by being flawed enough as a human being to make lesser poets feel that they could be even better than he, but above all, he did that by returning to his view that only fools and uncivilized folks would fail to see the value of poetry to society. The poet was engaged in a holy pursuit. Every lyric poet needs to have a hint of Dickey's dogged faith in verse, and our poets all show signs of this. Only a poet would assign himself a task as monumental as this when introducing his poems: "My hope for my poetical self is that I in some small way can help build a bridge over the abyss, to help reconnect the art of poetry to its elemental beginnings." The last person I heard trying to build a bridge across impossible time spans was a politician. Horace had a similar idea—an idea that Eliot would echo in his dictum: "In my beginning is my end"— when he suggested that humans could only function and make progress with a belief in what some have curiously translated as the "make believe" of a beginning.

Dickey's faith clearly seduced another of our Southern male poets, John Lane. A gentler man than Dickey, Lane is clearly echoing Dickey when he invokes Gregory Orr in saying that "a life lived from poem-to-poem can bless us. Save us even. Poetry can bring order from chaos. It can create for us a map to live by, an emotional landscape to inhabit." If poetry can save us, then only a fool would question the value of poetry. Of course, the people most likely to announce the salvation available in poetry are poets—the choir, that is.

Susan Ludvigson's idea of what the poet does is tied to this question of its human usefulness, but she is less convinced of its holiness than are some of the male poets. The reason is that she sees poetry as something of a savior that may not always be the most holy or pure—a kind of flawed savior. Poetry is about masking at some level—masking as a way to cope. "It's my belief that we don't change very much emotionally, even though we mature and learn to manage (and mask) what we feel in order to present a less vulnerable face to the world. I'm not certain that's a good thing for our souls, but of course it helps us get through the life outside ourselves. I think this idea—that we remain subject to childhood's raw emotions—runs through much of my work even up to the present." The poem, then, is a way to cope with failure.

But it remains personal failure, and for the most part these poets are especially interested in justifying poetry along the lines of a personal relationship with it—i.e. an evangelical vision of poetry—what it has done for "me," the poet. Angela Kelly, for instance, regards a poet as one who needs to have this opportunity to order life according to his or her whim or, as she says, "to impose your own version of reality." For her it is liberating to "give credence to what you like or remake whatever interests you by simply putting words on a page in an order designed to please only you, the poet." You see how quickly we come back to the poet as God. No wonder Plato had such basic problems with the poet.

Robert Cumming shares much of this faith in the power of poetry to transform in his own introduction. He begins with the important notion that the world is divided into two basic groups: not Jew and Gentile, but poet and non-poet. The poet, he suggests, deals in a world where "mental things alone are real," whereas the non-poet's "main trade is in objective, daylight things." There is something deeply tautological about this assertion—a kind of impossible assertion to disprove. After all, if a person who has long regarded herself as a non-poet were to admit that she finds that mental things alone are true, a kind person would be able to tell her that at heart she is a poet, she just did not realize it. There is a Calvinistic determinism in this idea that has the clever irrefutability of faith. Yet Cumming fully believes that poetry is a powerful entity, so much so that he borders on hyperbole in his attempt to contain everything that poetry can do. "Sometimes poetry wants to reshape my mind, sometimes to reform the world, sometimes to suck on sugar candy." And he ends his brief essay with one of the clearest articulations of faith in poetry: "Maybe any poem worth writing or reading confronts you with such concentrated image and language—such distilling of real, mental things—that it disrupts your conventional, half-distracted way of being and asks you to question your direction, even to begin again." One cannot be blamed for hearing "born again" in the cadence, rhetoric and syntax of this statement of faith.

Of course, not all the poets would be comfortable with this "religious" reading of their relationship with poetry. Despite this, one can't avoid that the pressure for usefulness in poetry is quite great, and, ultimately, it leads to statements about the human value of the art—that the art makes us better people or makes us understand ourselves the more. Warren Slesinger puts it in terms not unlike those we have come to expect from the very American, pragmatic approach to personal psychology: "It seemed to me that if I pursued it, if I inquired into it, I might learn something about myself and the world. I know that motivation is no measure of success, but I believe that I matured in the process. At least I am able to see myself more objectively and the poem more subjectively as a means of discovery." By submitting to the poem, the poet finds in it a tool of discovery. This quest to discover or to uncover meaning, whether through dream or through the attendant processes of making poems is part of the mystique that poets often will not undermine as they talk about their poetry.

It is curious and fascinating, then, when you meet up with a poet like Paul Allen, who is doggedly determined to convince us that his poems have absolutely nothing to do with helpful things like healing or personal transformation. After all, he assures us, his poems have nothing to do with anything that he may be "personally going through at any given period of [his] life." He declares with characteristic confidence: "The blank sheet of paper is not my psychiatrist's couch. ... The poem doesn't give a damn. The poem doesn't care whether I am happy, healing, sad, loved, abandoned, or bi-polar; it has no truck with my feeling close to or far away from God; it is completely uninterested in my divorce."

Of course in his very act of denying any humanity in the poet—in what seems to be a determined act to demonstrate that the poem is wholly a thing, an object, an artifact—Allen speaks of the poem as a person: a thoughtless, self-centered and human person, of course, but a person. The problem is that Allen is a poet and he is enough of a poet to imagine that a poem can talk. Allen, clearly, is an agnostic poet—he has a suspicion about the mystique of the poem, but he is unable to fully immerse himself in belief. He is, however, enough of a believer to regard himself as a slave to the poem—as a kind of vehicle through which the poem articulates itself. Allen toys with the Platonic notion of ideals in his sense that there is some essential and whole idea or poem out there which he must reach for. It is all, despite his efforts to strip the process of mystique, quite magical and mysterious.

John Ower, too, appears to eschew the idea of the poem as a statement of some lyric psychology reality—at least he says this of the haiku selections he chooses to include here instead of the poems he wrote before 1998, which he describes somewhat dismissively as having "some artistic merit. However, I have come to regard them as being 'overwrought' on both senses of the word [meaning, one assumes, emotionally indulgent and overworked as pieces of craft], as morbid and primarily of psychiatric interest." One can imagine this "loss of faith" happening in the face of the lean and quite un-lyrical strictures of haiku. The haiku attempts to be nothing symbolic, metaphorical, or especially ideological. It seeks to subsume the ego and allow the artifact of the poem to stand out.

Cathy Smith Bowers, however, is a former unbeliever who is startled somewhere on her road to Damascus by a light that blinds her into faith. She admits to once sharing Allen's entrenched skepticism about the capacity of poetry to heal—the idea of the writing process as therapy. She would "cringe," she says, at the very suggestion from her students that poetry was therapeutic. And then in a moment that carries all the hallmarks of the reformed soul, she announces: "I came to realize it was I—not my good students—who was, after all, the misguided one." Beyond this, she grows thoroughly spiritual in her articulations. Thomas Moore, in *Care of the Soul*, convinces her that "writing poetry is a kind of chronic prayer, a way of looking closely and lovingly at the mythologies of [her] life to realize, as Moore asserts, that 'the beast at the center of the labyrinth is also an angel.'"

And so with every religion comes a series of beliefs, doctrines, do's and don'ts that ultimately reveal the chosen from the damned. While Cathy Smith Bowers identifies the polarities and unbelief in direct reference to the poet, Carol Ann Davis has developed her own sophisticated way of distinguishing the blessed from the damned by looking at the poem, and, ultimately, by discerning the "purity" of the instinct that shapes the poem. Notice again the manner in which the language the poet employs is so rooted in the language of faith. For her, those poems emerge out of some egotistical urge to make poems. Those that grow out of the prompting that says, "I call myself a poet, I should be writing poems," are poems that, for her, emerge out of a kind of legalistic, old dispensational urging—an instinct completely void of grace:

> But those poems, coming as they do, from the conscious world of what I should or shouldn't do or know, don't offer much up in the way of revelation, and surely don't reckon with things (read truth, the world, big ideas, what have you) beyond the treacherous realm of the ego. They try to get the world to look at them, to notice their cleverness and reach ...

The poems that belong to the chosen few are those that "are interested themselves in looking at the world, glimpsing something, rendering that thing until it is plainly seen by all. In such a moment, the poem disappears, the poet is long gone, and the world, in its splendor and its grit, becomes a sort of offering we are privy to all at once."

We must not, therefore, miss the religious implications of this suppression of the ego—this disappearance of the poem. But, as with evangelical Christianity, it is virtually impossible to eliminate the ego. Indeed, the ego is a dogged presence that has to be battled until we die—that is the struggle of faith. Some poets avoid this religious idea by offering a more secular and pragmatic use of poetry related directly to the ideas of history and society. In many poetic traditions, most notably those in northwestern Africa, the function of the poet is wholly communal—the poet is a public figure who speaks for the community and carries within the history of the community rendered in verse.

Jessica Bundschuh only flirts with this idea, but still wants to retain her lyric sensibility. She speaks of her work of excavating from the detritus of history, narratives that must be salvaged by poetry and, by so doing, be preserved and cherished. "Poems," she says, "about the 'self-in-history' probe the way personal narratives are caught up on broader, societal events that define an era." Much of this promises to speak to the idea of the poem as a vehicle for the preservation and interpretation of history, which is a decidedly political function. But Bundschuh will not let go of the lyric—the personal. Such that a poem about a historical moment—a persona poem, even—"allows the poet a great deal of room by expanding her own memory." Bundschuh, then, wants to be constantly inserted into the work, curiously because she does not want to assume a "God-like" position over the action, but to be a "witness." Ultimately, she returns to the faith of the poet. Her book, were she to write one, would be titled, "The Poet as Witness"—a phrase she uses. Her witness, then, becomes something of an offering, and the poet is part of some larger religious dynamic. This idea of sacrifice or offering is tied closely to the rituals of sacrament, and Curtis Derrick shares a belief in this function of poetry. He describes poetry as "something of a sacrament that [he tries] to partake of daily." Indeed, of all the poets collected here, it is Derrick who spells out this idea of the vocation of poet as something of a spiritual, even a religious, life. He confesses, "I've gotten progressively un-churched and yet my spiritual life has deepened because of poetry."

Left with their introductions alone, we could be forgiven to believe that poetry is a profoundly mystical thing, a thing that transforms the individual making of the hearer and the reader something quite new and remarkable. But we would also be left with the distinct sense that poets are different, that they belong to some group of peculiar creatures who see the world in a different way and who are convinced of their unique and peculiar calling. When a poet tells you that a poem has changed his or her life, it is hard not to search for this transformative force in the poem. When a poet tells you that a poem simply took over the writing process and took him or her to places that she or he has never been—a world of surprises, risky undertakings and heretofore unimagined revelations—one can't help but seek out such powerful authority and magic in the poems.

And when a poet keeps reminding us of the deeply personal nature of the poetic experience, the sense that the poem is somehow mining experience and emerging as a fundamentally subjective engagement with meaning and experience, we can't help but feel that we are witnessing something as holy as the rituals of a Christian church—an evangelical Christian church more defined by the intimate connection with deity in the self than by a communal and catholic sense of ritual and tradition. Even when these poets try to evoke a sense of tradition, they remain inscribed in the idea of the lyric poet—the poet who finds meaning in the self—the poet, then, who values above all, the idea of self as first and most important audience. The reader, the listener, is an incidental figure in this experience. The reader and listener may gain something from the poem, but ultimately, the poem begins with the spiritual experience of the poet.

As a poet I almost fully identify with the instinct to cast the poetic moment as such—to mystify it or to read mystery in it. After all, we are a collection of prophets who are rarely declared to be prophets. We must almost impose our prophet status on the world—somehow work hard to remind them of our value. We are embarked on a tragic romanticism that sometimes leads to a terrible frustration because the art we make has an uncanny way of standing up on its own and being something quite different from what we intended.

I expected to find something that would link these poems together—some theme, some stylistic inclination, some mode and sensibility. I suppose I wanted to find something here that would allow me to talk about these poets as South Carolina poets, as if that title would offer meaning, a kind of distinctive quality that would separate the Palmetto State poets from the poets from other states and regions and countries and cultures. I may have even wanted the poets to speak of their poetic mandate as being related to their connection to the soil, to the state itself. John Lane seems to have done that, and it is clear that Ron Rash understands his function as a poet to be that of one who comes to understand the language and culture of his society and, in the process, to articulate that, forming, as he does so, a vernacular for his tribe—a process of writing his community into being.

But they are alone. I have to dig deeper to find threads. There are some: a certain self-deprecating humor that grows out of people who, at some level, understand what it means to be the defeated, the laughed at, the ridiculed. We see that identification with the underdog in so many of the poems—a kind of southern fatalism that is as much rooted in defeat and loss as it is in an almost genetic evangelical Christianity. And then there is a wonderful fascination with landscape—a fascination that never succumbs to romanticism. It is a hardy sense of the terrible beauty in nature—a quality that reminds us constantly that at some basic level, South Carolina is one large rural community wrestling with the meaning of its relationship to the landscape. You will find poems that will teach you the names of trees and flowers and rivers, and those will remind you that the people who live here feel connected to and at odds with this landscape.

These poets all seem to be of the view that they did not work really within a constant thematic line of engagement—that they could not be pigeonholed. However, it is in their articulations of what a poem should be that we begin to see something interesting and something worthy of extended study in the work of these poets. It is clear that caught up in a world that is so anchored in the idea of the Christian Church—a quality that renders this region part of the "Bible Belt"—these poets have developed a sense of their function as poets around the idea of faith: of Christian faith. It is not that these poets are Christians. Indeed, most of them seem intent on reminding us that they are not, at least not in any orthodox sense. But they seem to have been unable to let go of the frame of faith. They have thus poured into that frame a belief in the poem. It is one that in many ways enlivens us, but, pleasantly, it is not always one that helps us to read the poems or understand the poems better.

I say "pleasantly" because I think that at the end of it all, the poets would prefer that we simply encounter the poems and hopefully find our way in the poems. It is true that given the chance to talk about the poems, they feel compelled to let us know that these poems are not whims but grow out of a deep sense of need, a hunger for honesty. Linda Ferguson sees the poem as something that emerges from a hole—a hole that can be a mirror, can be a place of self-discovery or a place of reflection. She sees the hole as a constant—a kind of need. The metaphor stumbles around, and Ferguson is never quite certain whether the idea of the poem's genesis as a hole works entirely, but what is clear is that this hole is a profoundly meaningful place for her, and she, like all the poets in this collection, seeks to be faithful to the poem. In this sense, the collection represents a worshipping of the poem—a kind of devotion to the demands of the poem. And at the core of that demand is a quest for honesty. That we know this is helpful, but not necessary. The poems may prove to be far more useful as we try to find our poets. I say they are more useful because at the most obvious of levels, the whole exercise is about the poem.

I have not set out to list favorites of mine, or to try to summarize what each poet is attempting to do in the work he or she has given to us. I have resisted this because I am not sure that this is the best way for you to relish the way these writers use language. I am more interested in the larger picture, the kind of assessment that allows me to say that here in South Carolina, the modern lyric poem—that is the poem that is rooted in the "I" and in the recovery of this "I"—is alive and well. I can also say that the collection tells me that those who selected these poets remain inscribed in a poetics that is consistent with the kind of poetry that we see dominating the contemporary American poetry scene. The introspection is intense, dogged, and unrelenting; just as the sincerity and quest for honesty is earnest and almost religious. Music arises in these poems subtly—in the form of meter and occasional rhyme, or in the sudden formal excursion or vernacular indulgence that we see, for instance, in poems by the gifted Ron Rash; in the most unabashed of the southern-themed poets in the collection, John Lane, whose "Sweet Tea" is a stubborn anthem in the vernacular of the South; and in the sustained stand-up-comedy-tight-rope-walk-that-makes-it-successfully-to-the-other-end verse of Debra Daniels, whose "The Olive Oyl Tapes" is a tremendous accomplishment. There is richness here, a care for craft in so many instances that we are left with at least a sense of the sacredness of what is being shared.

And yet despite my admiration and despite the pleasure I have derived from the anthology, I do miss a more pronounced African American presence. I miss the poetry that Al Young, the gifted California poet, believes has been missing from American poetry for too long—the poem about history, about issues; yes, the poem that

Stephen Corey seems deeply skeptical about in his "Abjuring Political Poetry":

> Some men will shoot an infant in the face.
> There, that's a start—near pentameter, even.
> Has the world been bettered yet, or your mood?

We have hints of more political verse, but our poets are scrupulous about what they have included. They have chosen to be quiet about their politics and clear about their sense of self. The good news is that the presence of these poets in this anthology demonstrates that at some level, poets are being supported, that at some level, we still believe that it is valid to give poets money to write what they want to write. And the hope is that this will continue, for, ultimately, these voices do offer to our sense of place and culture in profound and meaningful ways, and we are the poorer if we do not allow these voices to be heard.

For my part, I admire the commitment to the spiritual value of poetry that seems to emerge from this collection, because I know that at some critical level the language that is used here emerges out of the poets' desperate need for a way to express the value of poetry. I am reminded of Linda Ferguson's confession when she says, "sometimes [I] muse at how I spend most of my life searching for a synonym, the exact noun, the perfect sound." This collection is a quest for that kind of meaning and value through language. The essays may not have managed to settle the question, but the poems stand as a wonderful testimony, a kind of witness to what the poets are about. That we can share in this is a very good thing indeed.

*—Columbia, South Carolina*
*August 2004*

# PAUL ALLEN
## Poetry Fellow, 1989, 1997

"Select five …," my assignment for this anthology says. Easy, until I begin. It's not that there are too many poems to choose from—I don't have a large *oeuvre*—it's that there are too many criteria by which to choose. Do I select the five on which I've received the most compliments? How about five which make me look skilled, or smart? The five which show that obviously I am a Christian?—or the five which show that obviously I am not (probably the same five)? Do I have any that make me sound rich, handsome, and thirty? But those criteria are about me, and if writing poems has taught me anything, it's that *me* is too small to fool with.

But maybe selecting five is like writing one. The poem on the page is only a collection of doodles and scribbles that landed near me after I jumped from the cliff, threw the parachute of everything into the air, and plummeted through sounds and rhythms.

Two things play a role in my freefall. For expediency, I'll just call them the conscious and subconscious mind. The subconscious makes the pictures; the conscious makes the pictures appear.

On numerous occasions, I've thought, *This event (moment, scene, feeling) ought to be a poem*. Without exception, every time I've tried to get at a poem by way of the subject or content, the project has ended in failure, thrown away or shoved in a drawer full of probably-never-to-be-looked-at notes. For me, the images must surface on their own while the conscious mind fiddles with issues of craft. Syllable stress and duration, sentence construction, line breaks and such are the crone's mumbo-jumbo, the spell which brings forth the images that are the poem's content.

When the pictures appear, shades that they are, my conscious mind returns to test them, says, "Does that image fit into the rhythm you're vaguely sensing? Hey, these lines are heavy on *n* sounds in stressed syllables. Do you truly like them, or had you better get a couple of them to fall on unstressed syllables to keep them from sounding so garish? Is the metaphor logical (in its own way)? Does this image seem stale, stupid, self-indulgent, or dull on the 20th reading? If so, Mr. Big Time Poet, you can bet it'll sound like that to your reader right out of the chute. Better go back, Doc; you left a couple of sponges in the patient." But of course, while playing this game, other images appear, and the process resumes. It resumes, draft after draft, until no new images surface as I struggle with the sounds and rhythms.

In order for these conscious attempts at craft to conjure up the subconscious images of content, however, I must adopt a state of mind where everything is there, though unformed, invisible—perceived as a sense of pure space.

It's an exercise in faith. Though I cannot see them at the outset of a poem, cannot see them until I play with sounds and rhythms, I know that the space, the pure nothing, is actually made up of every tree I've ever seen, every piece of broken glass I've stepped on, the eyebrow of every priest, the smell of every book, the cough of every dog, the taste of every nail and lover. And not just those from my experience—any I've ever heard about, seen on TV or in movies, read about in great tomes or on bathroom walls. I don't think up the nouns and verbs of content and then struggle to articulate them. I play with articulation and then receive the nouns and verbs.

So, what was I thinking when I wrote this or that poem? I was thinking, *I feel a kind of dum-dada-dum-o-ah-k-de-dum sound here. Wonder what syllables, and eventually words, fit that?* I can explain why I kept the ns in a line; I can't explain why there's a washing machine on the front porch.

Therefore, as far as I can tell, what I am personally going through at any given period of my life has no bearing on the poems I write. The blank sheet of paper is not my psychiatrist's couch. And I have friends and family who worry about me "as a person." They are interested in how a day or a moment impacted me. They care about whether I "find myself." That's the job of shrinks, family, and friends. The poem doesn't give a damn. The poem doesn't care whether I am happy, healing, sad, loved, abandoned, or bipolar; it has no truck with my feeling close to or far away from God; it is completely uninterested in my divorce. The poem says, "What is that to me? Your ways are not my ways." My moods and life-experiences may determine how many poems I write in a given period, or even whether I write at all. But once I start writing, I can't see that my moods or experiences have any direct influence on a poem. Maybe my psychiatrist, family, and friends can see it, symbolically, but I wouldn't know anything about that.

The poems I've included here were not chosen because they show my moods, artistic periods, best work, range, or any other criteria I might consciously adopt. So I reversed my original game plan and wrote the commentary first. I simply made the leap, flung all of my poems out into the air, and fell through the language of these remarks. The poems here are the ones that happened to land nearby.

▲ ▲ ▼ ▲ ▲

Born and reared in Selma, Alabama, poet and songwriter Paul Allen lives in Charleston, South Carolina, where he teaches poetry writing and writing song lyrics at The College of Charleston. His books include *American Crawl*, which received the Vassar Miller Poetry Prize (University of North Texas Press, 1997) and *The Clean Plate Club* (Salmon Publishing Ltd., Ireland, forthcoming). His poems have appeared in numerous journals, including *Northwest Review, Southern Poetry Review, Poetry Northwest, Ontario Review, New England Review, Iowa Review, Puerto Del Sol*.

## ONE UP BY CLAYTON

Upstate they handled drought their own ways
this year. They broke off corn stalks, picked
clods and winnowed them through their fingers
on all three major networks, and *Nightline*.

One up by Clayton used a .22 to make
a hole over his left eye. The half-
hour it took him to die, he slammed
against the étagère, knocked the clock

with the passage of scripture off the wall.
He fell to the rug, got up. He held on
to the latch and bent over at the back door
for at least a minute, like he was thinking,

like he was studying the dull boards
in the floor, how they were starting
to separate. He went outside and wiped
a cobweb off the post that was coming loose

on the porch. He sat on the last step.
He walked to the gate, dropped his wallet
through the grating on the cow-catcher.
He crossed the road and leaned on the Bixby

mailbox, hard, then died in the run-off.
There wasn't any mystery to it. On the local
stations, his friends knew exactly what happened
by what he broke, or smeared—where he'd started to bruise.

*1988*

# AGAINST HEALING

*He who lets go in his fall*
*Dives into the source and is healed.*
—Rainer Maria Rilke, "Elegy"

Original sin, my ass.  In the beginning
the earth was whatever darkness was, and wet—
was Anne, say, a widow (wouldn't you know it?)
at the end of the road who took you to her bed. ...

That stuff you've read about:  Chopin on
the record player, Orpheus holding a vase
across the room.  The birds and bees loved
her leaves around that house, her wild world
of shadows on surfaces, pockets of light deep in.

You would come to crawl among all that,
to kill birds (and bees)—bb's.  You
would come to be found out, to be brought in
for music, maybe wine, hear your shot
roll down the magazine when she disarmed
you at the door.  She took your shoes.  She led
you to the sink and washed any blood off your hands.

But her music never demented you like your own
loves later did: several ravenous decades
leaning into any magazine, or Delacroix
(*La Liberté guidant le peuple*), those round breasts,
and your eyes' fall to the patch of hair
on the cradled corpse at her feet.

For all of it, you haunted beaches, showers, flowers
on surfers' trunks, or closer to the pier you wandered through
bikini areas, thumb prints on your shades,
trying to look like you lost your book,
or your invalid mother. You began to like
*Bay Watch*, *Beach Blanket Bingo*, summer Olympics.
You're the one just off the I on every business trip
who tore out pages of the yellow pages
(BOOKS, VIDEO, MASSAGE, CLUBS)
or if they were gone with some kindred spirit,

you'd take TATTOO, BUS, PAWN, CHECK CASHING,
narrowing down the neighborhoods to cruise.
You wound down all the exits leading in
among the streets' ghosts, those most pitiful *least-of-these*
where you finally believed you belonged.  Isn't there always
a section of any strange city where you know you are home?—
where you know, in the smells and yells and bad acting
and money exchanged (shirt pocket to shoe) you belong—
just this once you belong, and this once, and this once.

Look, let's face it: By the time we feel
the need to heal, our standards are shot to hell.
We wouldn't know *well* if we could custom-order it.
No, you can't put that off on Chopin's song,
or even Adam's fruit torte.  Come on, to get better
you must name all the animals, and you have missed one:

Go back to that Motel 6 again.  Check in.
Stand naked as the day you were born.
There in your original-sin garment of animal skin
examine yourself in the streaked mirror with an eye
for love.  Step back: hair all over's going,
skin's drying; your veins have burst into bright pattern.
Why, you're no ordinary, garden variety man
who cropped up back in Anne's bit of wilderness.
You're serpentizing, Old Pale Scales.
I'm not sure you'd want to heal
before  you witnessed that.
I'm not too sure you can.

*2000*

# "All I Want for Christmas is my Two Front Teeth"

One of the few teeth that stuck it out all his life
sometimes gets away from him.
Trapezoidal, chalk-white, bright, and out of line,
it overlaps its little yellow brothers,
looms there like a monument,
like a cliff face in his face.

This is no tooth for a choir—
some "Living Tree" in a church.
It is a tooth that has written little more than a name or two
maybe 50 times in its life; that accepts driving tickets
without even looking back, as though to see the infraction
taking place,  says *sir, mam* to people half its age,
minds its business, stares at floors in waiting rooms;
a tooth that shuts doors to stores lightly,
that keeps the light off with women,
that finds women who have downcast eyes.

He is not a fool.  He sees in the populace
how they take it into themselves, or on themselves,
and knows from their eyes: Once seen, it's in their lives
and in their children's lives.  They may wake
to the thought of it themselves, as he has always done,
or use it to make their children eat their fruit,
*I saw a man once with this big, white tooth*
*in front. ... neglected his apples ...*

When all the *Theys* were young, and he was young,
they laid him on a turd near the flag at Byrd Elementary.
And when he cut out for good as a man,
a man gave him a ride, gave him 50 bucks
to let him do this or that.  Then something changed
the man.  He backed out of the offer, apologized
for even saying it, then begged him to keep the money
just the same.

It was the tooth.

He has always known it
whenever luck (or no luck) slapped him in the face.
When people notice it, they get that helpless look
of one more time not knowing what to say.

So mostly now he tries to keep his lip zipped
to spare them, spare himself, let everyone off the hook.
Except in seasons like this, when he feels called,
compelled by the time of year or the air, to walk
among them with a weird feeling in his heart
and gut and groin.  He moves along familiar streets,
the sky an angel blue, and all down-town busy,
though hushed—despite the tinny carols
hissing on every corner.  He passes
through the shadows under the snaggled awnings,
pauses between them in the warm shapes of sunlight,
and smiles at perfect strangers
in the spirit of the season.  And for spite.

*2002*

# THE BOOK OF THE RIVER

### I

Look, you don't just roll this life on,
do your business, pinch it off your shriveled soul,
and sling it out the window down at the boat ramp.
Kid comes along chunking rocks, sticks the point of his stick
into the rude lip of it, flips it high
to worm out of the sky onto his cousin's shoe.
Flood comes along one day and lifts it like a strip of newsprint,
takes it down stream, around the bend
into the branches of an uprooted tree.

### II

Then that summer we drift.
Mother's in the bow of the boat.
Dad works on the stalled outboard.
Like every frustration on every trip,
his arm and neck swear a sweaty:
*This is not my fault.*
Somebody moves the ice chest.
We don't care if he hurts us, mind—
steps back on our foot, pinches our fingers
when he shoves away the day's gear—
it is only important that he doesn't know,
he tries so hard.

The current delivers us to the leafless tree.
Motor's coughing.  Nothing sounds
more like two men going at it
than a boat getting caught
in the upper branches of a dead tree—
Daddy's *unhh*, *wha?*, *unhh* when he turns,
catches the edge of the boat with his forearm,
falls back, and the crack of brittle branches like ribs.
Easy, slowly, slow and easy, *crack*, ease deeper™
into the tree.  We all look at Momma,
her head bowed like it's going to be chopped off,
and there, hanging over her head like a snot
is your nasty Goddamn life—hanging there, and she bowed.
We all see it at the same time, together pretend it's not there.

Daddy grabs the paddle, skulls back, back—
back-paddling against the weight of a river so heavy
whole towns use it to name roads and views and law-offices.
Now what can a man, even a grown man,
do against something like that?
All we can do is wait for the tree to finish giving in,
and give us back to the river as though saying
*I think that's enough for now*.
Motor starts, and we fly down stream
toward the rest of the day,
Momma in the high, planing bow.
We have a good time.
You don't have to worry about that.
We have a good time, and come dusk, get back home.
We've never mentioned it.  But don't you go thinking
for one minute that we have forgotten
your little glorious ugly in our lives.

*1998*

# GROUND FORCES

We are the new militia, armed with empty arms,
inducted now by having come to know
the last shall be first and the first shall be last—but
concurrently. All those pleas—*God, Please*—
then hushed we hear ourselves swearing in:
*Well, I'll be* and then begin to be.

When Moses gets his huge oh-by-the-way
from Yahweh: You will see but not get in …
he clucked a little *Well, I'll be*, and was—
went back to star charts, rams' horns, faced the music
in the voices of schlemiels who still had hope
that they could live God's odds, husbands saying
—trying to say—wives saying—trying to say—
*It will be all right, honey.*
*Moses is using his snake rod, sea's parting.*
*I'll take the baby. Now please, try not to say anything.*

But maybe some—more than we might guess—
bathed themselves in the beautiful peace
of utter, complete defeat and stepped through the walls
of ocean water—just no point in staying home
and washing the blood off the door.

And like them, all those guys
who owned the pigs full of devils, all those pigs
sent spinning over the cliffs into the lake,
their livelihoods—their lives—bloating below,
(This Jesus getting wowed by those who loved him)
climbed down for one last look. They saw
they'd put their money on the quinella of wrong
animals on the wrong cliff at the wrong time
in the wrong land. Like the nation before,
they stepped to high ground,
saw in a moment of bright relief
that the cosmic brass ring
was bolted to the pole in any case.
They clicked their tongues to their mounts,
laughed a little *Well, I'll be* and shook
their heads, amazed they'd let themselves hurt

—and hurt their loves—through so much hope
and wanting all that time.

So each goes home, pulls his hewn stool
to table, not sad or afraid anymore, says:
*A god came along today and threw our herd
into the sea. We may have to tighten our belts.*
And she, does she rail? No. She is blessed
with the gift such knowledge is—touches his head,
her hands soft with grain dust one more day,
streaks of evening in the smoky room showing
the edges and angles of make do she has always
known. She laughs a *Well, I'll be*, and he,
knowing it is all out now—out and over—
loves her, laughs with her, and finally
the two begin to be. A victory.

See? Winners aren't blessed because they win
nor win because they're blessed
—Get it Hiroshima? Get it Cherokee?—
they win because the losers have been blessed.
Publishers' Clearing House, application,
resume, query, manuscript, bid,
bio—So, what are you waiting for?
Go on, send it in, Mr. or Mrs.
Strong-work-but-there-were-others;
Oh you, you Hope-you-try-us-again.
It isn't called submitting for nothing.
If you don't send, there's no one for the other
guy to beat. Any jerk can lick a stamp
or call cold contacts when there's hope.
You, the blessed, must try again precisely because
there is no hope. Your duty, graceful loser,
your final knowing it's going nowhere
means you must plug on from here on out.
You have been chosen to send it,
because you have been chosen to take it—
on the chin, again. And again.
And all those "goals and objectives"
(which you've missed), all those Saturdays
of making lists, pockets full of prospects, self-help books:
presumptuous to include them here with lives
in wilderness and ruin beyond measure?

Exactly!  Now you're getting the idea.  You
may be one of the blessed.  Another year
or two of this, and you might say your own *I'll be*.

If you've managed to stay among us,
friend, till then, not suffered death or success,
then join us. We meet often—
shaking it off, rubbing our chins,
chuckling in our tiny, blessed defeats.

*2001*

# JAN BAILEY
## Poetry Fellow, 1993

In selecting these five poems as representative of my work, I have tried to show four things really: variety in theme, language, locale, and origin. I have included a poem about childhood and one about motherhood, a love poem, if you will (these three set in the South), a poem which tries hard to capture the small forest on Monhegan Island in Maine where I lived for some six years and now live in summer, and a poem about getting one's life back after depression.

"Cathedral Woods: giving thanks" and "Maggie on an Upswing" take risks with language, pulling the reader, I hope, into the flux of the situation itself. I want the reader to actually feel the complexity of nature through diction, to sense the ongoing decay, the darker side. And I want the reader to experience, through language, the often-dizzy rise out of sadness. "Encounter" takes it slower, does not try to build word upon word, but is more interested in the event and its effect upon the mother. Hence the couplets. Couplets force us to take our time; space is time. In this older poem, a new mother languishes over her baby, turning him this way and that. I want the reader to slow down, to experience the examination, to perhaps glimpse this sudden difficulty at separation. "With What Wild Hand" arose from an actual experience in Cleveland Park in Greenville. My dog was swimming in a small stream pool when a snake appeared from the rocks, a tiny flapping fish caught in his jaws. Fifteen minutes later, and I would have missed it. The snake couldn't care less about my witness; it was going about its life, but I did feel blessed. I had no idea the poem would move toward "desire and devour." This totally surprised me—wonderful when it happens.

I will also have to say that my poems have different origins. Both "Encounter" and "Maggie on an Upswing" were givens. On my way to Atlanta, years after my son's birth, I pulled over to the shoulder on I-85 (was I nuts?) and scribbled the poem out on a paper bag. "Maggie" came full-fledge while journaling, from the sheer joy of writing again after long silence. "Cathedral Woods" is another story: That morning, I set out to write a poem. I took notes while hiking the wooded trails on Monhegan Island. "Bag of Promise" is right out of memory.

Surprises are best. Sometimes, for example, I am unsettled by my sensuality. Occasionally folks are embarrassed by my poems, but I don't mind taking risks if the emotion is honest. I don't mind writing about a swing up from sadness, or the longing to be engulfed, or the confusion children feel, probably much more than we know. And this is exactly why I love poetry—because it is always new, experience reinterpreted, language honed and precise, because it gets at what is real and so forgivably human in us all.

▲ ▲ ▼ ▲ ▲

Nominated three times for a Pushcart Prize, Jan Bailey is a winner of the Elinor Benedict Poetry Prize from *Passages North* and the Sue Saniel Elkind Poetry Prize from *Kalliope*. Her latest collection is *Midnight in the Guest Room* (Leapfrog Press, 2004). She serves as chair of the creative writing department of the South Carolina Governor's School for the Arts and Humanities. She grew up in the foothills of South Carolina and holds an MFA from Vermont College.

## BAG OF PROMISE

She never could refuse him though he shamed her–
years of peddling life insurance to the lame,
the outcast, the overextended, folks so
beaten down by loss and mayhem they'd forgotten
how to bypass the absurd, and so Saturdays
and holidays she rode along, checking off
his list of clients, past shanty farms and scarecrows
long crucified by wind, sheds spray-painted to
Serve The Lord Only, tire swings and outhouses,
hounds bound with chunks of chain to tired front steps.

He had the gift of washing guilt clean off her
face like a magician who sweeps his wide hands
over the eyes and pulls a penny from an ear.
And when he'd ease back into the car, hat cocked,
a smudged contract and smelly bills balled in his
fist, it was to her as if he had hand-delivered
Santa to the front door and dumped a bag of promise
right there by the woodbin and the sorry sack of coal.

*2002*

# CATHEDRAL WOODS: GIVING THANKS

for the strands of web that wet
my cheek, the autumn ash, its blast
of crimson berry; for the red
belted polypore, the spotted
collybia, the old man's beard
like woolly wire; for hunch-
backed boulders bearing upon their
shoulders small sprigs of yew;
for slag water sprinkled with leaf,
its funky perfume; for roots
gnarled into knees and roots
bowed into questions I trip over
as I scan the tall spruce, a hopeless
fool for crows; for the braided
rope of felled trunk, a leviathan
laid out along a meadow frail
with weeds and brown fern;
for all the wounded trees
that succor lichen, the spit
and snarl of broken branches;
for November sky, low, low
and layered gray; for the rain
pools, their time-warped reflections;
for the dull sparrow, the junco,
the cardinal in her dusky coat
and cap, the female jay;
for the half-blown carcass
of a gull wedged between two
rocks, its tiny nave of ribs
picked clean; for the maze
of blue mussels, fodder for ducks,
the coins of mottled lichen
along the ridges of the rocks;
for the dispassionate, the dying,
the unbecoming; and for my longing
to be unraveled, unnerved, undone
until I am gray air, sea, stone.

*1993*

## Encounter

When the nurses left the room and his father headed
for home, I lay him in the crook of my right arm

where he fit like the wing of a wren. I untied the gown,
released the diaper and then I slid downward in the bed

until my face faced his, to drink the white aroma of his skin.
I sniffed behind the flap of ear, the crinkled neck.

Beneath the bowl of arm, the side, the inside
of thigh, the foot and each toe, I languished.

I smelled the knees and lay my face quietly between his legs.
And then I turned him. Not once did he cry out but stared

with that blank blue of contentment. With my tongue
I traced the dip of his back, kissing each buttock.

Had I been braver, I would have licked him like a cat.
I wanted to; wanted to take first the heel, wanted

then to run my tongue along each toe, wanted the nubby
hands, the curve of elbow, wanted even the wounded

penis, wanted to swallow the small seedcase
of his body, to let it lodge beneath my ribs,

to let my thin bones grow around it, wanted
to make him then and forever mine.

*1985*

## Maggie on an Upswing

What is this drapery of sun sheen,
this Oz overture through psychedelic poppies,
this heyday razzmatazz unhinging door
I am bulleted through, wearing my wild grin,
resurrected and spanked clean.

And what predawn conversations
helter-skelter in the trees before I dare
open my eyes, no longer filing through
my list of the lame–efficient nerd clerk
of censure in my high-boned collar and tweak tie.

What dishrag of dry tears dare I press
and fold away, what empty lines pen in,
what worn rug of grief from bed to TV
roll up and singe, what dog bone of old
shame may I give permission to bury now
that I am (say it!) hopelessly happy to draw
back the blinds and burn my dark eyes green.

*2002*

# WITH WHAT WILD HAND

Out from the crevices of the rocks
amid soda cans and Styrofoam, he

skimmed the shimmer of the pond
and toward the waterfall, a flapping

silver fish clamped in his tight snake's jaws.
It had just begun to rain and it seemed

the willows fanned further out, away
from the canopy of oaks.  I stood

transfixed as he glided with such grace,
his head regal, intent, a boasting head,

the fish quiet now, and I the gaping
audience, though I doubt he knew it.

All day I felt the spectator and slower
my pacing and watched the world lean

toward love.  Desire and devour.
In the quick of an eye the toad unleashes

its tongue, a cricket stills.  We know
the story–gristle to bear, and in the muscled

sinew of lion, the sleek flank of gazelle.
Just now I licked the salt from your lip,

your brow and swallowed your salt kiss.
It is dark, shadows are eaten–no blouse

across the chair, no stockings, no floor.  To where
am I pulled, into what pool, with what wild hand?

*2003*

# CATHY SMITH BOWERS
### Poetry Fellow, 1990

---

I used to cringe when I heard my students, after a few days in my creative writing classes, exclaim, "This stuff is great therapy!" I would, after an attempt to regain my ruffled composure, gather myself into my most academic voice and correct the unfortunate, misguided assessment of my life's work: "This is not therapy. It is art!"

It was not until I read Thomas Moore's *Care of the Soul* that I came to realize it was I—not my good students—who was, after all, the misguided one.

It is in this astounding book that Moore reminds us of Socrates' pronouncement that therapy "refers to service to the gods." I came to realize that for me writing poetry is a kind of chronic prayer, a way of looking closely and lovingly enough at the mythologies of my life to realize, as Moore asserts, that "the beast at the center of the labyrinth is also an angel."

The ostensible beasts I usually confront in my poems are things I have lost or do not understand. "Snow" and "Mother Land" deal with the subject of my greatest emotional investment, the complexities and mysteries of the biological family. Both poems surprised me as I watched metaphor emerge from simple and literal descriptions of abiding images. These two poems represent the point in my writing life at which I began trusting the metaphor to find its own way into (or out of) the particular experience I was exploring at the moment.

"Orchids" and "Learning How to Pray" are representations of the darkest time in my life, my youngest brother's courageous struggle with and subsequent death from AIDS. It is a subject I will never stop writing about.

"You Can't Drive the Same Truck Twice" is a poem that taught me that the feeling we might have thought we were dealing with in a poem was not what emerged at all. I wanted to write a poem poking fun at my first husband's impossible old pickup truck. When the line "I loved him for his love of broken things" emerged, I realized I was, instead, writing a love poem to the kind, gentle boy who years ago saved my life.

Whoever said, "No surprise for the writer—no surprise for the reader" knew, indeed, what he was talking about.

▲ ▲ ▼ ▲ ▲

Cathy Smith Bowers is the author of *The Love That Ended Yesterday in Texas*, *Traveling in Time of Danger*, and *A Book of Minutes,* all published by Iris Press. She teaches at Queens University of Charlotte in the low-residency MFA program. She lives in Tryon, North Carolina.

# MOTHER LAND

I pitied the other children
their skinny mothers. Nothing to burrow
when the church pew began to harden
like sugar-brittle or God. Their elbows
sharp as crags we climbed to the bluff
where Jimmy Adams took our dare
and jumped and never came up again. I pitied
them their mothers, all point and longitude,
tentative as sandbars the chain gang
dozed to stay the river banks. My mama

was a continent, terra softa
where she sprawled in her big chair
or across the bed when thunder ripped
the shingles and rain swelled the sills
like ripe earth. And there in the valleys
of blankets and pillows, each of us staked claim
to whatever fleshy region we had chosen to settle
while the storm spent itself. My sisters
nestling the soft slopes of her breasts, me floating
meridians of hip and thigh. My mama
was promised land and we, small redoubts
not even our father could penetrate, odd denizen

from that country of men we could see
mounting the horizon, their bright
flags flying, their cannons aimed.

*1992*

## ORCHIDS

No wonder my brother
in that year of his life
began peopling his cliffside home
with their strong and delicate
tenacity          began foraging
the genealogy of their loveliness
as if they were kin

ancient aphrodisiacs
aristocrats of sepal and stem
star-children of the orient    it is
this story he loves best
forgets twice he has told it
and tells again   how once

in old New Guinea       a Belgian
expedition and their native guide
startled upon a show of sweet Dendrobium
sprung from a mound of skulls
ribbony wreaths marking
the forgotten unhinged door
of fontanelle       each bloom
half bird       half spider
not quite furred breast
and breath of bumblebee

on the last morning of my visit
he called me to the mirror
by his front door       said look
as he lifted his shirt and stared
at his own reflection       I touched
the flesh around each lesion
as if to validate the freshly
tilled soil of his body
then looked up

past him     past me
to the mirrored space
behind us     to his quiet
anthem of orchids
whose seeds store no food
who can     if they must
survive on air

1997

# SNOW

It was the only act of intimacy
I ever witnessed between them—that joke
my father told her, his opening
line…I hope it snows so deep…and then
how, for the punch, he reached out
and pulled her to him, to whisper words
that sent her red and slapping
at his khaki shirt and then her hand
lifting to his chin to remove
the little ghosts of cotton
that fluttered there. Our teachers
had sent us home from school calling
See you Monday that Thursday in December
as we ran crazed into the schoolyard
and to our separate houses
to hold vigil for that white coming,
that promise we wanted so badly to believe
we could feel, already in the graying
sky, its soft descent. All evening
the heater roared its warmth
into the room as we talked
of snow-cream so cold it hurt
your head, the fine spin a hubcap gives
down a hill of white. But by the close
of second shift, all that had shown
was a stray, barking beneath
the streetlight, our father in from the mill,
blowing the night from his hands
and telling that joke, his mouth burrowing
into the smell of our mother's hair,
and somewhere, breaking dim above the smokestacks,
a few odd stars no one would admit to seeing.

*1994*

## Learning How to Pray

When I heard my brother
was dying     youngest
of the six of us     our
lovely boy     I who in matters
of the spirit
had been always suspect
who even as a child
snubbed Mama's mealtime ritual
began finally to
pray     and fearing
I would offend
or miss completely
the rightful target of my pleas
went knocking everywhere
the Buddha's huge
and starry churning     Shiva
Vishnu     Isis     the worn
and ragged god of Ishmael
I bowed to the Druid reverence
of trees     to water     fire
and wind     prayed to weather
to carbon     that sole link
to all things
this and other worldly
*our carbon who art in heaven*
prayed to rake and plow
the sweet acid stench of dung
to fly     to the fly's soiled
wing     and to the soil
I could not stop
myself     I like a nymphomaniac
the dark promiscuity
of my spirit     there
for the taking     whore
of my breaking heart     willing
to lie down     with anything.

*1997*

# You Can't Drive the Same Truck Twice

*for my ex-husband*

When I heard the sudden
thunder of my husband's truck
explode into the drive
and saw him, after ramming
the defective gear-stick
into neutral, emerge crazy-eyed
and fevered, fling up
the battered hood, go down
and disappear beneath its open wound
of primer, I knew how the evening
would go. How deep into moonlight
he would hang like Jonah, half in,
half out, his full weight given
to the wrench, gripped to the stripped
bolts and nuts, capping and uncapping
the ancient battery, his body
lost to that odd carcass of scavenged parts.
I loved him for his love of broken things—
the handleless hoes and axes, the sprung
rumble seat bought years ago
at auction, the legless chairs
retrieved from garbage heaps,
that truck each day he reinvented.
Like the rivers of Heraclitus. Like Van Gogh's
olive trees and irises that quiver,
still. Bristle. As if caught forever
in the antique instant of their opening.
It's why we love Jesus, some philosopher
once said, instead of God. Why lovers
love the moon that's always falling.

*1997*

# JESSICA GRANT BUNDSCHUH

## Poetry Fellow, 2001

As a poet, I feel challenged by John Milton's dictum at the beginning of *Paradise Lost*: "Heav'n hides nothing from thy view." Such a freedom drives my interest in more spacious forms like the long or mid-length poem; in fact, "Juniper Berries" is the beginning section of a longer poem, "The History of Gin." It has been my project to understand how the lyric moment and narrative time intersect in such a form. Further, the form of the mid-length poem allows me to set the personal in relation to the social.

Poems about the self-in-history probe the way personal narratives are caught up in broader societal events that define an era. I am particularly intrigued by moments in history that are outside *my own* memory, but within a single person's memory. One of these poems, "The Routine of a Letter Writer," is a persona poem; the artifice of a persona certainly allows the poet a great deal of room by expanding her own memory. Especially interesting are those memories on the verge of a larger, more public event that would fade away if a poet did not memorialize them. Maybe that is a bit of what "The Tsar's Daughter in the Forensic Lab" does—this figure, the Tsar's daughter, plays an important role in one of the first blood baths of the twentieth century, but this forensic lab and her posthumous interaction with the forensic examiner do not. It's the side story, but for me that's the main story.

Likewise, in "A Reader's Habits," while Napoleon's exploits on the battlefield are well-known, his reading habits are not. Hence, the poet's task is to dust off that forgotten moment. The last poem of the five, "Open Like a Vowel," demonstrates what I think is most important for the poet, that is, to be engaged in the world in front of her. Even if I create a persona, I try not to let myself be a narrator, removed and absent from the action. While Milton's dictum perhaps implies a God-like position, above the action, what is more interesting is that as a poet, if you're willing, the world will open itself to you. The beauty, then, is that the poetic epiphany must arise from simple observation—the poet as witness.

Jessica Bundschuh has published her work in *Antigonish Review*, *The Paris*

*Review*, *Quarterly West*, and other journals. She spent 2002-2003 as a guest lecturer at the University of Stuttgart as part of a Fulbright Lecture Award. Before leaving for Germany, she served as a visiting instructor at The College of Charleston and was an assistant editor for Crazyhorse. She has an MFA from the University of Maryland and a doctorate in literature and creative writing from the University of Houston.

# Juniper Berries

> For beauty is nothing
> but the beginning of terror…
> —Rainer Maria Rilke

Fear is what quickens me.
To steal juniper berries from heaven,
from the hands of these blueblue
needlelike branchlets, to break
the oil glands on the leaves—to inhale.

It all begins in terror.
For me that terror is found here:
a girl waiting, upon waiting—
her mother a cold cook, her father a waiter:
I am the girl who waits in the windowless
back room with the companionship of Frangelico,
the monk-shaped bottles of hazelnut liqueur
I memorize the way another child
might Aunt Jemima at the breakfast table.
Ever waiting.

I am like the girl who dispenses straws and chopsticks
at the Chinese takeout around the corner.
Sometimes she opens and closes the door
until she is shooed back to the chair
beside her mother and the cash register.
She learns from her mother how to sit still.

I am a girl who waits, one who knows
the taste of drawn butter gone cold,
butter meant for dipping artichoke leaves.
I am the girl who knows the pulpy texture
of romaine saturated by Caesar dressing—
a salad my father in his tuxedo made tableside
in a large wooden bowl, a task he performs
like an orchestra conductor in the main dining room.

My mother prepared his score in the back:
filleted anchovies, 1/2 a lemon wrapped in gauze,
a dash of salt, an egg, romaine, parmesan, croutons,
and the big pepper grinder they bring out

with the flourish of cracking gold on lettuce.
I want to be the woman who orders
a double Caesar for her main course—
weekly she comes to watch my father's deft hands.
I can only imagine him squirting the lemon
with a fury, liberally pouring out the olive oil.

It begins here: this picture of a girl,
you could easily forget, leaning into a bush,
smelling the aroma of berries born to yield gin.
With uncomplaining patience, I wait
for the remnants—raw silk at the end of a ream—
of what others have left, scraps bused
from the tables. This is how I developed
the adult taste for béarnaise, for cold filets of beef,
for hearts of palm, for anticipation, for neglect.

It begins here: I hide among the bushes
circling the Black Canyon restaurant
in this mountainous town
at the base of the Rocky Mountains
where all the blue columbines hide.
I fumble with the dark and spicy juniper berries.
They are purple and hard as pebbles—
the white waxy chalk rubs off on my fingers.

Juniper berries survive neglect.
They survive best in the bitter winds
where Greek navigators can see both
the Crimean and Anatolian shores:
the tip of the cape, wind swept and rocky,
is lush with juniper that waits stranded
and admonishes the weaker vegetation it shelters
farther back, saying: Leave me the steep rock;
leave me the cassia bark, the coriander,
the cardamom; leave me the Black Sea,
its water churning in small caves below my rock
that radiates red on a sunny day.
It is my fate to be your wall.

Such a cape is where the Romanovs
built their palaces, the cape of Ai Todor
shaped like Neptune's trident. Here the wall

of St. Peter looms, its face a sheer drop in the water.
And, here, juniper alone survives the rough
company of the Romanovs: Sandro, Nikolasha,
Peter, Dmitri, and Constantinovich,
their constitutions well suited for the dry malt
of gin: introduced to England by soldiers
returning from Holland. A survivor's drink.

The Romanovs, though not survivors
themselves, understood the props of survival.
The last Tsar, Nicholas, read Sherlock Holmes
aloud to his wife and children.
It must have soothed him to imagine
having a Watson to interpret his adventures,
to polish his faults to a cognac luster,
to tell his stories long after he's gone
over the cliff in his enemy's arms,
Watson, the posthumous interpreter who makes
even a cocaine habit charming: a protest
against the monotony of existence.

Surely, standing there in front of that juniper bush,
I wanted a sidekick too: brave and faithful,
balancing my coldness with his warmth,
solving the mysteries of my life inductively.
As a detective might, I begin in observation:
out of the ordinary particulars of juniper berries,
I come to understand history, beyond this girl,
terrified that the waiting won't stop, and, that even
if it did, there's perhaps nothing to wait for,
no reward for the sweetness of perseverance.

*2002*

# THE TSAR'S DAUGHTER IN A FORENSIC LAB

He's made her ordinary, spread her slim
seventeen years across this table,
measured her tight little head,

pieced together seven-hundred bits.
There's a box for her femur and pelvis,
and one more for her ankles and vertebrae.

There's a foot in her jaw, a bayonet
above her ribs, a drill-press,
an anvil, a wrench. There's a saw-blade

embedded with diamonds like those
in the corset she wore under her dress,
diamonds sewn so close together

she almost survived. And there's her jaw,
its sharp corners moistened
seventy years later in the center of his lab.

She's older than this glossy green room,
air chilled so breath fogs a microscope lens,
colder than bones on top of cabinets,

already boiled free of their flesh.
He loosens his collar, warns us
of bones boiling dry, drains clogging.

He says, My field is human bones—
my last case was a massacre,
a tub of children's bones

lit up, it seemed, like many orange flares—
it might have made her smile
before this slow minuet

with too few men, before
that basement slaughter, poised
at once for any photograph.

*1998*

# THE ROUTINE OF A LETTER WRITER
## *NAIROBI*

I measure breakfast in a tin cup
for a morning at my stall by the P.O.,
a bench of rotten wood, my station.

My English transcriptions are not
like those of my dead predecessor,
an Indian scribe who swept a sender's

Kikuyu into the lingua franca of Swahili,
or marshaled into a hybrid English:
Some fire came into my house

and ended one excellent goat, or,
I got newly female infant by my wife.
My routine is not extraordinary:

a lift of my eyebrows, a twist of my neck,
right ear out. I set my client's words
in an old tradition, even if his confession

consigns my fingers to burn lead—
lies about one bloody massacre,
one forgotten wife, one flood,

one tantrum that led to the ripping open
of a lover's blouse and a claim:
she just woke up that way, screaming.

1998

# A READER'S HABIT

I remember that departure.
Mohammed, an Egyptian neighbor who only gave gifts of leave-taking,

thrust a copper-lidded bowl, compact & curry-colored, into my hands, saying,
It was Napoleon's ashtray in my country.

On my kitchen table its utility disguises its history, made more plausible
since I discovered Napoleon's reading habits:

Instead of letting white sheets flap to & fro, like prisoners waving kerchiefs
for attention!, or listening for the patient

sing song of its proofreader, its message hammered out through black ribbon,
then punched into type on slivers of hot, hot lead—copper atoms sparking—,

the Emperor pitched it from his carriage's window.
The book simply did not please,

did not cram him with adventure, or mystery, or romance.
Today the books he read in transit, those dust-filled creatures

spine-broken below one too many wheels & gathered up by fellow travelers,
fill the catalogs of Parisian booksellers,

a testament to how he cherished an ashtray's heft, ugly & tarnished,
—a lover of cheap snuff & sweetened table wine—

over the consistency of a book, which must have certainly slowed
the heart-drum of this discontented riffler.

The one he read in his study after dinner suffered all the more cruelly,
not far from the bonfires to come later;

yet those books would bear the mark:
forbidden & lawless—oh! the excitement in being mistrusted—

& Napoleon's was just a bore, felicitous kindling
thrown lightly into a low-lit fire, intoxicating           itself.

*2000*

## OPEN LIKE A VOWEL

On an afternoon walk to no particular place, a small stack of pebbles lies
at my feet. A small stack of pebbles I hadn't noticed yesterday.

I would tell their histories to any lover: looking into his blue or brown eyes,
explaining how they bounced along the riverbed like words in a sloppy sentence

or the sentence of a speaker nervous because she's being too real,
pebbles worn round and smooth by abrasions, no place to go but downward, to the ocean.

I would tell the story slowly as if it were my own, my mouth moving cautiously,
opening each vowel like an egg, or— I don't want to say something ridiculous—

like a refrigerator door, and my lips open, pulling out the last rrrrr sound.
He certainly would see my pleasure in making this sound—raunchy, rough, like motor
          revving

and my tongue suspended in the middle of my mouth like a guilty lover's.
But we're talking about pebbles here—what I particularly love is how gray they are,

all of one color. I would bend to pick up a pebble, a smooth one, and taste it—
running my tongue across its surface (finally it tells me its salty history,

how it came from the sea; how it had no mother, no father.)

*1996*

# STEPHEN COREY
### Poetry Fellow, 1982

One cannot speak honestly about his own art without sounding to some degree arrogant, which is why speaking only *through* the art is nearly always the best course. But making the remarks that follow was not my idea, and so I am freed up a bit.

My five poems here seem to exhibit a couple of qualities that are important to me as I revise and reconsider my work: First, they have managed to come as close as I could possibly bring them to being what they proved, during the composition process, that they *needed* to be. Second, they are—unlike the preceding sentence—wide open to the comprehension of readers and listeners without being superficial or simplistic.

Poems pursue different ends (I told you this would have to sound arrogant). "The World's Largest Poet Visits Rural Idaho" is built around and upon an idea, however fanciful and silly, and despite the poem's profusion of physical images the core remains an intellectual/aesthetic one. "Quilts" seeks to capture a voice—a voice very far removed from any in which the poet would or could ever speak in his "real" life. To me, and for me, this effort to become someone else is one of the most difficult goals I undertake as a poet. Usually I can't manage it; I believe I got to it in "Quilts"—which is of course a kind of love poem, though one very different from "Who Would Not Seek the Perfect Gesture of Love?" The latter tries to grasp the ungraspable, the most complicated of emotional nuances, and it cares for nothing else. "Abjuring Political Poetry" is another idea poem, but here the idea is *made of* images rather than illustrated by them (as it was in "The World's Largest Poet"). And the concept "Abjuring" tries to hold onto is just as elusive in its repulsiveness as love is in its marvelousness. "To My Daughters at My Death" is another mood-based piece, yet weirdly tied in with the intellectual as it tries to imagine the ultimate unimaginable—nonbeing.

So, now you must cast aside the long paragraph I have just given you, and read the poems. What I think the poems are doing does not matter to your reading of them, though my belief that the poems have successfully followed their lights does matter for me. Also of great matter to me is whether you as a reader can find a way into these poems. I believe that you can, basing this belief on the reactions of prior readers. If you cannot … well, then, you can probably save yourself the trouble of seeking out others of my works. If, however, this literal handful should prove to your liking, please read on elsewhere, for you may find more of interest. I just thought you might do well to begin with these: little, ring, middle, fore, thumb.

▲ ▲ ▼ ▲ ▲

Stephen Corey is the author of ten poetry collections, most recently *There Is No Finished World* (White Pine Press, 2003) and *Greatest Hits, 1980-2000* (Pudding House Publications, 2000). Individually, his poems have appeared in *The American Poetry Review*, *Poetry*, *The Kenyon Review*, *The New Republic*, *The North American Review*, *Ploughshares*, *Yellow Silk*, and many other periodicals. He has been three times named author of the year in poetry by Georgia Writers, Inc., and he has earned fellowships from three state arts councils (Georgia, South Carolina, Florida) and from the Bread Loaf Writers' Conference. Since 1983 Corey has been on the editorial staff of *The Georgia Review*, based at the University of Georgia. Associate editor since 1986, he recently served as acting editor for several years. In 1976 he co-founded *The Devil's Millhopper*, an independent poetry magazine, for which he was co-editor and then editor until 1983.

# THE WORLD'S LARGEST POET VISITS RURAL IDAHO

His 300 pounds on his 6-11 frame
will not fit into the dean's VW
waiting at the bus station. He must wait again
while a forty-mile round trip brings another car.

At the Pine Tree Motel, the world's largest poet
piles baggage on the underlength bed,
naps on blankets on the tile floor.

That evening, a low table his only podium,
he ducks and squints to read his poems.

Both he and his hosts are aware of all this.
They have him for the glaciers and wild birds
That spring from his giant fingers.
He's there because the battered humming
in his head will not stop.

*1977*

# QUILTS

*One woman wept, they say,*
*when a peddler reached her cabin*
*with no new patterns to sell.*


*Irish Chain, Persian Pear, Rose of Tennessee*

I still make my bed with *Kansas Troubles*—
I was only five when Mother said,
"Twelve you must have in your hope chest, before
the Bridal Quilt, and that before you'll wed."
First my stitches tried to mirror hers,
our hands touching as we worked.
At night she plucked mine out
to keep her project whole.
Next came simple sewings: double lines
and scallops on my own crazy quilt.

*Bear Track, Turkey Track, Beauty of Kaintuck*

Some days, when Tommy and Jimmy ran outside
shouting off the chickens, I thought
I'd stretched myself across that frame, waiting
for the womenfolk to pad and quilt and bind me.
Yet with all the years of work,
when the time came Joseph had to wait
seven months while I finished Jacob's Tears.
The Bridal must be perfect, Mother warned.
A broken thread, a crop gone bad;
a twisted stitch, a baby dead.

*Wreath of Grapes, Flying Swallows, Pomegranate Tree*

Sometimes our life is no more than the names we give:
Joseph moved us to Missouri,
and the women loved my *Jacob's Tears*—
but they knew it as *The Slave Chain.*
In the Texas flatland winds, *Texas Tears*
lay across the bed, and after the last move

we slept warm beneath *The Road to Kansas*.
That was many droughts and storms ago.
The colors still blaze enough to shame
a Puritan, and not a seam has given way.
Joseph is gone, but even coldest nights
my *Kansas Troubles* brings me through till dawn.

*1980*

# Who Would Not Seek the Perfect Gesture of Love?

Never was there anything enough to say…
yet once there I was,
watching the back of your head
and the left side of your jaw line
from my seat behind you on the crowded bus
as you gazed out the window,
there in that time when I was
brought into your presence, by our work
and by chance, for a week after years
apart, years of what they call nothing,
but of course was unable to touch you
since I had no rights in the world
outside of our fractured hearts—
and as I watched, a stray blacksilver hair
waved and swayed apart from the rest,
a cracked limb dangling in wind
like the wand of a fairy or the scepter of a priest
offering its foreign blessing
to one who dares approach.

I reached over the seat back; you still stared
away. My hand passed above your right
shoulder and alongside your neck,
opposite the window. I caught the thread
(younger and smarter I'd have called it *angelic*)
in the pincer of two empty fingers
to lift it away—a tiny blemish,
a flaw that could float on air.

*1999*

## ABJURING POLITICAL POETRY

Some men will shoot an infant in the face.
There, that's a start—near pentameter, even.
Has the world been bettered yet, or your mood?

The only mirror of horror is itself.
Art's a game when it thinks it shows the world
in actuality; art's a savior
when it stalks the world as art: stone as stone,
paint as paint, words as the music of words.

Here's a joke we children laughed at once:
*What's the difference between a truckload*
*of bowling balls and one of dead babies?*
*You can't unload the balls with a pitchfork.*

It's okay to laugh—that shows you sense the awfulness.
Imagine the hearer who did not get the joke:
No poem could reach him. No horror. No world.

*1988*

# To My Daughters at My Death

Forgive me for grouping you again—
I have never done so lightly,
would speak to you singly now
if such would make more sense.
But I know you are gathered
in that clutch we made of you,
that clowder and murder and pride
we failed to see we were building
in the shine of all that we loved you, one by one.

Yet I am not here, and am not here
to say such glowing, tinted things.
You are reading me, I've guessed,
as a breathing quartet—four of anything
or a group engaged in music…
but there I go again, averting
even my dead eyes and trying
to divert your pooling thoughts
from this one sheet and all of me
you hold in hand. And hand. And hand. And hand.

The matter, I feel, is this:
what did I withhold as I tried to give,
what broke on the circles I presumed to close
with this second language I learned
when the first, my life, became a spell
too convoluted for my breaking?
Did I turn from you in the paltry name of art,
diminish you for the silly sham of wisdom?
My wise beauties—
          Heather of hardy flowering,
          Miranda of vision and wonder,
          Rebecca of searching and strength,
          Catherine of purity—
                    my wise beauties,
where have we left ourselves now that we're possessed
by the separate worlds we'd only feared or ignored,
now that I have no hand to touch your hands?

So much I missed of all you did and thought,
but now I miss it all: raise or lower your eyes

in trust or question or anger, and remember
I will not see. And wonder, can there be such sights
wherever I might be now? Do I still know
the shading and shift of light in the delicate iris?
Pray for me, who never taught you how to pray,
that such a chilling, shivering thing might be.

*2000*

# ROBERT CUMMING
## Poetry Fellow, 1982

Maybe for poets especially, what Blake says in "A Vision of the Last Judgment" is true: *Mental things alone are real*. Non-poets whose main trade is in objective, daylight things need a mask of consistent purpose. But for me anyway, what I do in and want from poetry—shadowy mental things—varies wildly. Sometimes poetry wants to reshape my mind, sometimes to reform the world, sometimes to suck on sugar candy. Resonance matters more than a given content. So—as far as subjects go—there's not much consistency in my writing, or in the following poems.

"Storm Light" reflects the experience of a midnight lightning storm with my wife Deborah, in our farmhouse outside Greenwood, South Carolina. During this period I was becoming aware of a deep gap between the reasoning, discursive mind which I usually assume directs my life and the mind of the senses and the imagination which goes its own way.

"Sleeping in the Abbey" reflects visits to the vast north-England monasteries—Whitby, Rievaulx, Fountains—which were abandoned to ruin by Henry VIII. The architecture and the rites which lay behind it seemed alive, even in the face of dizzying physical and cultural deconstruction, even in the face of us casual backpackers trekking through. And the repeating sestina form which the poem took on seemed right to record that recycling.

"Like" came to me out of the blue, more like whimsy than forethought. The off-the-beat rhythm and images may say something about a way of looking at things different from our usual categories and rationalizing—poetry's way.

"Looking at the Land" reflects the slaughter of the Carolinas' countryside. It's easy to blame the developers and politicians; I've gradually woken up to complicity in myself and other seemingly uninvolved, nature-loving people. I admire and want to write poetry which deals with the commonwealth. Politics needs poetry's inward-directed eye, which can detect—in the temper of individual lives—blindness, bravery, inspiration, corruption and other sources and outcomes of public happenings.

Like some of the earlier poems I've included, "A Ship" draws heavily on a dream. Dreams seem to be the surest source I have for poems: they tell more certainly than ideas or even experiences what I need to get at in writing.

This dream seemed a forewarning of the need for change—even a massive disruption—in ordinary life.

So maybe there's more consistency to what poems I try to write than I'd recognized when I began this introduction. The poems I care most about are dangerous: they challenge some part of the way I usually relate to the world. This is why poetry is uneasy-making: however alluring, it threatens. The poets Rilke and Rich have said it: *you must change your life*. Maybe any poem worth writing or reading confronts you with such concentrated image and language—such a distilling of *real, mental things*—that it disrupts your conventional, half-distracted way of being and asks you to question your direction, even to begin again.

▲ ▲ ▼ ▲ ▲

Robert Cumming received a Fulbright-John F. Kennedy Foundation fellowship for teaching and translating in Thailand: this led to the publication of *A Premier Book of Contemporary Thai Verse* (translated and edited with Montri Umavijani and Deborah Cumming). He has also published poems in *The Chattahoochie Review*, *Southern Poetry Review*, and other magazines, as well as in the 45/96 collection of South Carolina poetry. As a student he was literary editor of the Harvard *Advocate* and the Oxford *Isis*; his education continued in the Suan Mok monastery in Thailand and the Satsang ashram in India. He has taught at colleges in New York City, Thailand, and South Carolina (Lander University). Currently he lives in Davidson, North Carolina.

## STORM LIGHT

White.  The window's gone white.
In the night did they paint it white?
But it flickers.  Panes tremble.
We're stripped of our sleep, our cover.
Now thunder.  Somewhere else,
now here.  Hear it hover,
now crack.  Feel it quiver,
now bristle, smash all over.

I turn in bed towards you, my twenty years' lover
and catachist.  Shall we get up, go to the window?
There are questions we have not yet asked each other.
This storm intrudes on us.  We're not yet ready,
we must know ourselves.  What was it we believe?

We kneel at the window.   We are neophytes.
We've never seen that bush before.
Black.  White.  Black.  Pure shape.
Trees appear and disappear.
Negative positive.  The old new.
Come wind.  Come fire.
We are acolytes.  The whole yard
shudders like a fragile altar.

*1993*

## SLEEPING IN THE ABBEY

The stone we're lying on stiffens.  I squint at an arch
fifty yards up. Like some dream in the mist.  No shelter
from weather.  Soon the sun and the Kodak sky
will make our sleeping bag sweat.  What is it we're hoping,
looking for?  The other arches have fallen.  No bells
to wake us.  Why stay in this place of dreams and failure?

Those first monks, half murdered by Danes, fled here out of failure,
clutching their teacher's bone.  They started an arch—
the hacked-out piers in the crypt—in lieu of bells
to ring praise to the saint's knuckle.  And to be a shelter.
A fortress.  A barn.  An altar.  Stones were their hoping.
They sang in the quarry, under Ezekiel's sky.

Joiners hooped a wheel that could hoist to the sky
stones to lock in high vaults, with no fear of failure.
A sculptor carved Gabriel's horn, emblem of hoping.
Painters strewed stars up the piers to hallow each arch.
Glassmen mixed sand with cobalt, color of shelter.
Smiths dropped gold in their vats to sweeten the bells.

Pilgrims climbing their last hill heard the sweet bells.
Caught sight of spires, flags streaming in the sky.
Knelt in the chapels.  Slept on these stones for shelter.
Found in the knuckle all freedom from guilt and failure.
All space and all time in the dark curve of the arch.
In the blue mother of God all grace and all hoping.

*Pig's knuckle!*   cried the King.  *As for hoping*
*peace from the fat priests, I want those bells*
*for cannon.  Many's the miser lurks under an arch.*
*Have at the walls.  Let the dim crypt see the sky.*
*Bowed hood hides idle head, heart's failure.*
*Knock the nest, wasps fly elsewhere for shelter.*

Only dreams, they say, can offer us shelter.
If I build you stone walls, they'll vanish like hoping.
Love's like faith, lazy and freighted with failure.
Where's the brittle knuckle, the fantasy bells?

The King's men tossed the flags out into the sky.
I want to say to you, here below the monks' arch:

Give up hoping.  Listen for stolen bells.
Give up failure.  Look for flags loose in the sky.
Give up shelter.  Sleep here, under this falling arch.

*1991*

# LIKE

Like not a real hike but a lazy stroll
hanging out too long at the corner in case
some longlost face changes her mind and
happens by or else somebody new
out of the blue shows up
with some new blue tricks to do
a poem needs to hang out and sniff
around like your thinbrain grumbly hound or
friend who can never understand
how to lick you goodbye or when.

*1992*

# LOOKING AT THE LAND

Spring-green oaks, gold hickories, sometimes
the almost black shape of a pine
hang like a net on the middle ridge.
Dogwood and judas-tree gleam through,
white and rose-violet.  On the ground,
clear as if he were there,
pillows of grass cropped round by deer.
Down the far slope through the laurel slick,
leaves glinting,  blossoms pink-white
as an arm, a creek seeps out of the soil
and runs,  he can almost  hear it,
over pale stones scattered in a curve
like stray remains from the knobbled rib
of some vast, long-ago beast or man
that lay on its back in the leaf-thick turf—
its marrow turned to water flows
onward into its riverbed spine—
to dream its last most perfect dream
of hawks and minnows and sycamores.

Closer, down at the ridge base, cut
into the dense bottomland dark:
an orange-red slash, like flesh scraped
and waiting for a surgeon,
glares in the windshield where he sits.
And two small bulldozers, like blunt
razors, push at the raw clay's edge.
In the space where the near ridge used to rise
he can see what the operation is:
slope shaved down, bottom filled up,
power lines hung, sewer lines dug,
big houses closed in by bushes and walls,
little houses strung out like fish on a line,
the whole place pocked and strapped.
Was there something he could have done?
The city grows, the suburbs spread.
He'd needed a car and an extra room.
The money was good.  He'd sold
his part of the ridge.

One high school fall his girl and he—
his eyes go higher, he's almost there—
climbed their old way through the still woods
up the shadowy slick by the trickling stones
to the ridge crest. They lay on their backs
in the pillow grass. She read to him
from a schoolbook: but because I am poor
I have only my dreams.
Holding the book her inside arm
was laurel white, her outside arm
was hickory gold. Tread softly, she read,
because you tread on my dreams.
They let the clouds drift over the trees
but knew, in a year from now or an hour,
they'd be lying in one another's arms.

Did she leave him or did he leave her?
He can't remember. Maybe it's something
both learned. At college they pretended
to forget. He bought a car one year
and sold his part of the ridge.
The city grows, the suburbs spread.
The whole world knows what it knows.
He married someone who'd had other friends
just as he had, someone who understood
how you give up what you once loved
for a car you need or an extra room.
Nobody sensible tried to hold on.
He looks across to the far ridge,
the one the bulldozers haven't touched.
He watches it sloping out of sight
while sun and clouds turn it bright and dark.

*1999*

# A Ship

A ship has come to the far pier.
Its shadow falls over the dockland below.
Ropes reach down from the high deck.
Vines—flowered, fragile—curl upward.
Each person must pull himself aboard,
shinning his way on one of the coarse ropes.
He may draw up a vine, to remember his home country.

Now?  Or is it too late?  My wife and child
help me pack, searching the old building.
But my clothes are lost,  strewn through the disordered rooms.
The locks are broken.  Others have moved in
their petty belongings.  There's no suitcase anywhere.

On the road to the pier I look back.
The building explodes.  It tosses bricks to the sky,
sinking into dust.

Ahead the ship strains
at its foot-thick hawsers.  Its hollow horn
travels out over the open sea.

*1999*

# DEBRA DANIEL
### Poetry Fellow, 1994

Some poems burrow under your skin and squirm there. The itching won't let you forget you wrote them. They are layered inside you, tissue upon tissue, all the way to your core. These poems cannot be sloughed away. As Olive Oyl says, they're strawberry-sized blotches. I am marked by them. They are deep in my skin. I want the readers to be there, too, so that they can see what is inside me, and in turn, somehow see what is burrowing under their own layers. That's a tall order, but that's what I hope happens.

I am a storyteller. If I examine my work, I find that I crave plot and character, setting and detail. There is a need to be grounded somewhere: sitting in a church pew, walking a deer trail, parked in a backseat. I want to watch poems like I view a movie—see the hula girl, the can of spinach falling on Olive's toe, a test tube of air captured by a vigilant son. I want something to happen in the poem, and I'm most satisfied when something happens to me when I read it. For the poem to resonate, something has to happen each and every time I read it. Every time.

These poems take me from where I have come and show me I am still there but also that I have surfaced. Here are the great awakenings: sexual temptation, the advent of war, death of parents, end of love—someone else's or my own. In all of them, there is some sense of loss. In all of them, there is nostalgia. And I like to think, there is some hope, too.

Why these five when I have left out so many others that tugged at me to be noticed? Because they would not stop itching. Because scratching them again was such a sweet relief.

▲▲▼▲▲

Debra A. Daniel was awarded the 2002 Guy Owen Prize. She has also been awarded fellowships in poetry and fiction from the South Carolina Academy of Authors, the Dubose and Dorothy Heyward Society Prize, the Lyric Prize, the Broulik Prize, and the Carruthers Prize from the Poetry Society of South Carolina. Her fiction has won the South Carolina Fiction Project prize and was included in *Inheritance: Selections from the South Carolina Fiction*

*Project* (Hub City Writers Project, 2001). She received a scholarship in fiction to attend Squaw Valley Community of Writers and has been a featured reader at the Black Cat Readings in Salisbury, North Carolina; the Savannah Poetry Rendezvous; and the Sundown Poetry Series at Piccolo Spoleto. Her work has been published in *Southern Poetry Review*, *Tar River*, *Gargoyle*, *The State* newspaper, and the *Charleston Post and Courier*.

# HYMN OF INVITATION

This spring they are in style again,
those piqué blouses with buttons in back,
the ones that bare the arms to day-lit nights,
nip the waist, then slit and flit to a coy hemline,
flirting with the earliest hint of hip.

I wore mine first on a Sunday evening,
vespers in a whisper-painted church,
sunset and colored glass in ripe reflection
on the boy next to me in the cushioned pew.
Slanted rays blushed him, stained his hands.

When the lights dimmed for the sermon,
he pulled a pen from his pocket, leaned forward,
drew on the length and meat of his thumb,
a hula girl; and as his knuckles bent and swiveled,
she danced a crimson sway.

His gaze angled at me, brown eyes
so humid, I wanted to lift my hair, let air cool
the nape of my neck.  He straightened, crossed
his arms so that his hands were hidden.  We sat
not quite touching, the service edging to invitation.

And then his index finger slow and sure as sin
found and grazed my sleeveless skin,
tracing a line down and up, down and up;
while the girl he had drawn lay folded
and curled tight against his palm.

*1999*

# EXHALING

*"Henry Ford somehow convinced Thomas Edison's son to sit by the dying inventor's bedside, clamp a test tube over his mouth, then plug it with a cork."*
—www.roadsideamerica.com

What could Ford have said to coax Edison's son
into dragging a straight-back chair
across the somber gray of someone's dying,
and not just any someone, and not just any dying?

What persuaded him to scrape the chair
and himself close, closer toward the bed
until he mashed into mattress so that he could lean,
bend over the old scientist, rig a way to fasten

the rigid coolness of tube to the open dry of lips
and wait, wait, however long it took, to capture
final breath and become fatherless. With that last
breathing, Ford believed, body gave soul release.

Why would any son steal his father's soul,
allow it to be kept forever enclosed?

In Dearborn, Michigan, visitors tour Henry Ford's
Museum where a sealed case, nothing more
than a waterless aquarium, contains that very test tube
still trapping the last of Edison.

What if I went to Dearborn, Michigan, with a smuggled
hammer or one of those glass breakers you keep
in your car in case you plunge off a bridge. And what if
security is lax enough that I can reach the case

where Edison's soul is entombed? What if I smash
the glass, open the tube, release that soul; or inhale it
myself, let the dying of Charles's father circulate
through my body's streams, let the breath

of someone else's parent merge with mine to be exhaled
into the cycle—oxygen, carbon dioxide—light and moist.

*2003*

# Hunting the Mine Hill

Covey busted, we search
for singles along the hedgerow.
Keeper flashpoints, then snuffles
through briar-lined pockets.
Scouting the patch of sicklepod
Ranger locates a deserted roost.
When he returns, the feathers
of his tail are cockleburred, snarled.

We follow a matted deertrail,
bending and edging to Hugo's ridge
where we stop and pay respects
to hardwoods lying in state.
There is plenty of cover here
for a bobwhite to hold steady,
to find place with pine cones,
to outwait the arrowdogs.

When we cross the creek,
Ranger laps, measured and sensible
while Keeper wallows, douses her belly,
flings muddy water, clambers up the bank.
One field over, squealy-mouthed hounds
hassle a rabbit, rattle the nerves
of a doe, but our setters work quiet,
only a belled collar marking their hunt.

At the highest crest, we drop
to the ground, lean against a loblolly.
The dogs doze undisturbed
by the drone of machines,
the rumbles at the mine
marring the clarity of winter woods,
the bare branches still defined,
uncluttered by spring's tangle greening.

*1995*

# Lottery 1969

Before our midnight curfew, our dates
would end behind the church, the darkest corner of the lot
where we would park in his father's car, allowing sin to swallow
truth, seduce the virgin moon we'd known before men gathered lunar stones.
That summer hummed a siren song, blew lyrics in a breathy draft
like liquid air from ripened plums that rippled on my cheek and neck.

I would languish in his arms, kiss-dizzy from our necking,
and as his fingers found the hooks I planned on how we'd set the date,
designed the curtains, bedspreads, wrote the rough draft
for our wedding. The navy sky, to me, was more than just a lot
of science. I was born a moon-child and the birthstone
I adopted was that silvered crater-face that hid its crescent swallow

of earth-born men behind its smile like Vietnam was swallowing
moist gulps of boys in clamping jaws. I knew that marshy neck
of land from correspondents in the field, from anchormen, stone-
faced, reporting: blood-washed news of body counts totaled to the date,
how unrelenting student protests led to votes for drawing lots,
how war-aged boys would curse their birth or celebrate the draft.

Everything was burning: rocket fuel and villages, draft
cards, bras, and flags. Sex was just a kiss away; drugs, just a swallow
for the thousands who'd dance summer in a farmer's empty lot,
and Hendrix's Banner song scraped his guitar like glass ground in its neck.
Beads and flowers, love and peace and hair—like prayers to validate
the faith they'd offered to the lyrics of the Beatles and the Stones.

But I was just a small-ways girl. What did I know of getting stoned?
For backyard boys afraid of war, it was for them, I feared the draft.
I'd lived a hammock life of football games and movie dates.
Those growling, fisted students drank spiked words too sharp to swallow.
I did not battle for the war, against the war, go neck and neck,
join sit-ins, love-ins, picket lines, face tear gas riots with the lot.

That sweet July we'd cool ourselves by walking in the parking lot,
a mask of clouds to fool the eye. We'd take small steps on gravel stone
or lean against the car and nest, his chest to cushion my head and neck.
Sometimes we'd drink a beer or two—illegal bought, a lukewarm draft.
The taste of it and him, of night and moon mingled as I swallowed.
And in the end all that remained was lunar dust to prove the date.

In December lots were drawn—his called early in the draft.
He sank deep as river stones, but I remained to play alone the diving game of swallows—to pluck a fallen feather from a curving neck of air and claim it like a birthdate.

2000

# THE OLIVE OYL TAPES

**1.**

Tossed with mandarin oranges, almonds,
bacon crumbles, freshly grated Parmesan,
and a citrus vinaigrette or as an hors d'oeuvre
blended with artichokes, sour cream and spread
on garlic toast points—those were my favorites.

Hours I spent scouring cookbooks for recipes
to please him, preparing omelets, soufflès,
egg rolls, lasagna, spinach burgers, spinach soup,
shrimp Florentine, chicken Florentine.

But his palate was as unsophisticated as those anchor
tattoos on his arms.  He ate it straight from the can.
Tepid.  Salt-drowned.  When we were dating, I was charmed
by how he kept a can in the glove compartment,
several in the trunk beside the jack, the spare tire.

"For emergencies," he said.  I laughed when he asked me
to stash one in my purse *just in case*.  Weekends, we'd scrounge
garage sales, flea markets to complete his collection
of can openers displayed in velvet-lined shadowboxes.

I'd find cans under the mattress, inside the ice cream churn.
Once I was bringing Christmas decorations from the attic,
a box tipped.  Everything crashed on my feet, breaking my toe.
He'd hidden a can in a stocking.  In the attic.  Heat rises.
It could've exploded.  I knew then he needed help.

**2.**

Pipe smoke gives me violent headaches.
Sometimes they last for days.
I lie in a quiet room, total darkness,
push in earplugs, and use compresses.
I alternate hot, cold, hot, cold.

For awhile I had chronic hives.
Blotches.  All over my body.
Strawberry-sized.  One, on my inner thigh,

I swear, was Bluto's profile.
That one I covered with a bandage.

The doctor prescribed steroids.
Pills, except for the acute attacks,
Then I got shots at the emergency room.
People tell me it's stress.
But it's not. I'm allergic.

## 3.
He calls himself a poet. Well, spinach and finach
do not rhyme. Poetic license, my ass.

## 4.
Popeye said the steroids would help me bulk up.
"I don't want muscles," I'd say the whole time
we were lifting weights at the gym. "Definition,"
he'd say. "That's what we're aiming for."

When we were younger, he praised my figure.
I could've been a runway model. I was 5'10".
96 pounds. I still am. How many women
can say that? Fellas were bug-eyed over me.

Pierre, for one. Voulez-vous coucher, don't you know?
I rejected him. What was I thinking? And Wimpy,
he wasn't after hamburgers. Popeye had no clue
how he offered to press my patties and butter my buns.

The real threat was Bluto with that reckless streak of his,
the storm waves of black hair. He went back to school,
got a degree in electronic engineering. His wife and kids
come through my checkout line at Wal-Mart.

## 5.
I'm not anorexic. I'm not bulimic either.
It's only when I eat spinach that I throw up.

## 6.
Pappy's in a rest home, thank god.
It's not that I didn't love the old grouch,
but he was driving me insane.

No control over his bladder or anything else.
He smelled like bilge water.  Every time I looked at him
I thought, *in twenty years, this is Popeye*.

**7.**
If I hear, "I yam what I yam," one more time,
I am afraid of what I might do.

**8.**
About a year ago Jeep
got sick.  He couldn't control
his bladder either.
We'd had him forever.
Part of the family?  Not mine.

Strange little thing,
more vacuum cleaner
than dog, terrorizing
the neighborhood
until finally we had him fixed.

Then he and Popeye
were just alike, sitting in the den
like a pair of stinky socks.
We had him put to sleep.
The dog, not Popeye.

**9.**
I know spinach is loaded with iron.
That's not the point.
They won't let him in airports, for god's sake.
He sets off the metal detectors.

**10.**
I was an honor student.  Too smart for a girl, they said.
The class voted me friendliest and most likely to succeed.
My nickname was Man Magnet.  I was just most likely to.

**11.**
Popeye hasn't worked in years.
He gets a disability from the Navy.

Doctors say his insides are rusting.
All that iron.

Every few months he goes on a tangent,
writing letters to Green Giant suggesting
they make him their spokesperson.
He wants his picture on the can.

## 12.
There is no twelve-step program
for spinach addiction.

## 13.
Sweet Pea spends hours at his computer.
He loves anything electronic, anything with a plug.
He can dismantle a radio or TV and put it together again
with his eyes closed.  He's a good boy, but Popeye
barely speaks to him now.  Once they were, well, like two peas.

It's perfectly fine nowadays.
Women have babies all the time without being married.
It's quite the style in Hollywood.  Women visit sperm banks,
for god's sake.  But it was different then.  It was taboo.
I disappeared for awhile.  When I came back, life went on.

No questions asked.  We said I was the babysitter,
Sweet Pea's nanny.  His parents, we told everyone,
were somewhere in Europe.  After awhile, the fact that he lived
with me was just accepted.  Maybe people gossiped,
but no one knew the truth, not for sure anyway.

Even Sweet Pea doesn't ask questions,
but sometimes when he's working at the keyboard
I stand in the doorway of his room watching
him think, watching his hands soothe the dark tidal
wave of his hair, and I wonder if he suspects.

## 14.
I can't remember the last time
someone shivered my timbers.

*2000*

# CAROL ANN DAVIS
### Poetry Fellow, 2004

There's a progression. Something in me, or in my sight line or hearing, catches, and I want to follow that thing as it moves forward, so I sit down, not knowing at that point what it is I'm after. I might have a line by the time I sit down, an image, or just a sort of tonal color (that phrase borrowed from music), but it's enough to go on, on faith, hoping that catch catches something else. It keeps going that way, one sentence to the next, before that, one line to the next, until the poem makes itself known, finds its own way towards unity, meaning, whatever you may call it. After that first drafting, I sit with the poem, revising it, giving it a shape and title, undergoing a sort of delicate negotiation during which I am set the task of listening hard to what the poem would have me do. I've learned to try to listen for that, because the good poems come from my listening hard, my drowning out what I think is right for this or that line and listening to the sheer integrity of the language, the pattern emerging of its own energy and made of its own stuff.

There are other types of poems, poems that grow out of situations or that stick close to memory, poems I begin so as to think through a problem and solve it, or worse, poems that begin because somewhere I thought, *That would be a good idea for a poem,* or, *I call myself a poet, I should be writing poems.* But those poems, coming, as they do, from the conscious world of what I should or shouldn't do or know, don't offer much up in the way of revelation, and surely don't reckon with things (read truth, the world, big ideas, what have you) beyond the treacherous realm of the ego. They try to get the world to look at them, to notice their cleverness and reach; the other type, the type I hope I've chosen for this anthology, are interested themselves in looking at the world, glimpsing something, rendering that thing until it is plainly seen by all. In such a moment, the poem disappears, the poet is long gone, and the world, in its splendor and its grit, becomes a sort of offering we are privy to all at once.

Or that's my hope. Each of the poems included here began with a catch that caught hold and moved forward.

▲ ▲ ▼ ▲ ▲

Carol Ann Davis's poems have been published in *Poetry*, *Double Take*, *The Gettysburg Review*, *The Southern Review*, *The Iowa Review*, and other journals. She received the W.K. Rose Fellowship from Vassar College, her *alma mater*, in 2000. She is assistant professor of English at The College of Charleston, where she teaches creative writing and edits the literary journal *Crazyhorse*.

## Ars Poetica inside an Evans Photograph

Because the book is still open,
the girl with the light eyes

stares at me
instead of into the canyon

of her brother's brow
on the facing page—

holds up the round head
and ellipsis of hat,

hair the color of straw,
straw the color of sun, such that

tiny shadows become black rings
at the photographer's feet. Ink on the underlip,

interruption, a word memorized
and called away. Nearby, boots

on a shelf, calendars reading
June-July-August,

the days no more consumed
than overgrown. Before long,

thoughts catch in the verticals
of the house's wood slats,

in the dust we are born to. Set to meet all
coming and going, the dark rims

of her coronas circle up
toward fine eyelashes. Just up ahead,

there's a rumor of rainfall
it's a test to disbelieve,

a season which turns to ocean
behind our backs.

*2002*

## AS ELSEWHERE,

this horizon slopes away to where
nothing's clear, its thin dime
stays thin, stares down the truth
of our innermost.  It soon disintegrates,
loss and likeness trading
their faded uniforms.  No matter what,
when the nurse comes home
from a double, crosses herself
at the threshold, then sleeps, dressed,
on the foldout, the traffic report
continues without her.  Trouble on the cloverleaf,
at the Vespers, at Montrose.  Who can say
when the afternoon quit
and evening began, or who would try,
shadows long on the wood grain,
on the standing lamp.  From this window,
you can catch the whole show,
V of geese heading up & back, the direction
the antique compass always points
from its shelf, how it replicates something
you'd be foolish to name.

*1999*

# IN THE ROOM

Outside, freeway and river
seem to balance out, each asleep

where real air hurries into tiny schools
to lick the claws of mangroves,

and he wakes up
from something very near
time beginning again,

my father's breath
startled, as if
it all could come back to him at once
in just under a minute.

He doesn't squeeze my hand
so much as worry
a familiar spot deep in my palm,

an old habit
just turned up in him,
one that signals
*I'm awake* because
he can't make a sound,

and if I'm lucky I look over
in time to see the underbelly of one blue eye

find its spot below the lid
where an imprint of the window
nearing orange

like the sun burned into the eye
must be.

*2001*

# GIACOMETTI PORTRAIT IN FOUR PARTS

I.  Man Walking Quickly in Rain

Let him begin there

and start what becomes
included in the history
of a thought.  Or better,
the wood his foot touches,
let it forget the shocks
and aftershocks.

Why shouldn't such a figure
immediately bring to mind
Pascal in his room,
before midnight, before
the conversion & breakfast,
when he sat in wonder
while a vacuum twirled
within reach of one
outstretched hand?  The slap
of a boat, rocking offshore,
is like a gentle slap of the hand.
And a shadow, in his case,
defined simply as a shape
(within limits) which intercepts
the light from a body.  Original rain
fell, the walk covered, glistening.

A man walking.  The thin line
his body makes.

II. The Evening Model

She sits in a straight-backed chair
and he does too
four feet from her, both
on their marks on the concrete,
the windows of the studio
looking onto a perfectly dark
passway. He has been painting her
for several years,
at this time of day,
in this light, though her changes
are marathon and nothing
will do. Her first kiss
took place in the afternoon,
and her meals are taken
well past dinner
to meet this engagement
she wouldn't miss. There are instructions
to look straight into his eyes
and the occasional HEY
when she finds a focal point
behind him. Above him, a rack
of abandoned figures; she doesn't think
*I am one of them*. She thinks
*I know those dark sticks*
*like the backs*
*of his hands*.

III. The Glade: Composition with Nine Figures

I want to ask myself questions.  Among them,
where have you been and how much longer
seem the most frequent.  These long fingers
of the imagination rest here
in a deep glade which dwindles
down to nine.

Nine starward trajectories, I think,
then think, no.  Nine colors
you can't see to look, light
forgiving us its nomenclature,
the past forgiving nothing.  These nine

have grown so used to each other, they seem
to lean toward or away according
to their mood.  Giacometti's moods
have quit plaguing them.  He's left them back
to remind us, a block set on uneven ground,
their universe not unlike our solar system,
except bigger.  You will think me strange
for saying so, I hope.  I hope
the world falls onto this page
and the last figures left standing are these nine,

and they forgive us.

IV. Reading a Letter in which He Tries To Explain a Famous Sculpture

A grove of pine twenty years later
becomes several men standing upright,
men swaying and thin, standing
in a proximity reminiscent
of a grove of trees in northern
Italy c. 1912.

       As if he stood
with a lab coat over his shoulders
and a lot of glass bottles pouring,
pouring until the big explosion.
Because you work a thing until
it shows you, what it has
inside.

       It's fall here, the ratchety engine
of a neighbor's car carrying through
clear air. The typewriter's keys
cause my landlord to tell me
knock it off.

       Alfred Nobel
with his powders, Picasso drawing with a lit
match, the war photographs which
help build this moment into an hour. You
will recognize something: the tree as it stands,
the light and the work it does.

*1997*

## Naming You

*—for my son, Willem*

Before you were named, you came in a white boat.
It was the first of many crossings
in which grief was nearby holding a little sprig

of olive.  It was a day with blind heat
and no small number of finches.  I mean to record
that in Siena the lily had grown imperceptible
on the church wall, rubbed to nothing

by believers in mortar, in paint.  I considered Indigo,
its long history, then ate some Chinese
which made me sick.  Like licking a stamp
to the nether world

or pasting illustrations to a letter
by way of worship.  Before you were named

I had a name for a little while, not long.  It was Dispirito
and went back after a week to its native land.  Before that,
Queens was Queens and the automats were filled
with girls from Macy's,

but most of that world is gone now,
my little map of sky, my archivist
of bone.  Now the 100 names for God
build a pile of sticks at your feet, if you have feet.

If you have eyes you know about light and dark
and the paucity of still rooms.  If you like, we can sit together

and you can run into the yard
when you hear the train coming.

*2002*

# Curtis Derrick
### Poetry Fellow, 1992

Choosing five poems that "best capture the range" of my work is difficult. Though in some ways my "range" is not that vast, I've been writing as long as I can remember, more than fifty years now. As a boy, the urge to write poetry stemmed from the usual mercenary impulse—the need to win favor with my parents and other grown-ups who loved me. Being both son and grandson of Lutheran clergymen, I was steeped in sacred rhymes and verses—hymns, Biblical passages, blessings, and benedictions. So immersed was I in the power of those words that I never doubted the power of my own. And so, writing alternate words for hymns or table blessings for special occasions had tremendous currency with my elders. The verses seemed to come naturally, and getting the lines to work metrically and in rhyme held a special fascination for me. Then, in my sixties adolescence, fate struck a mighty blow.

My high school English teacher, Miss Lacey, for whom I had a mad crush, made an announcement: Anyone who got published in *Spectrum*, the literary annual, would get an 'A' the rest of the year. Wasting no time, I finished a sonnet by the end of the period. Reading it, she gasped, "Oh my God! This is good!" For the entire last quarter, I basked in the radiance of her approval. She even gave me a ride once in her yellow MG with the top down. When the poem came out, it was the first time my poetic voice was heard outside my family. For that reason, I have included the poem here, just as it appeared in *Spectrum*, simply entitled "Sonnet." Reading the lines today, I'm struck first by how fitting a tribute it is, in theme, form, and musicality, to my childhood poetic pursuits. It strikes me equally appropriate as a jumping off place for what poetry has become for me since that time—something like a sacrament that I try to partake of daily.

In my twenties, my poetry became more personal and more secular. From that period, I have selected the poem "Gusta" about Augusta Petressen, who taught art to my brother and me. What she instilled in us about light and shade, image and depth, has informed what I know about poetic imagery too. I am always mindful of how our vision detects both positive and negative space, and how we use that which is visible to sense the invisible. As a result, tone, texture, and palpability are all goals for which I strive in my imagery.

In addition to images, a poem also evokes a persona, its voice. "Faith Nabors, Preacher's Daughter" was written in the early '80s when I was experimenting with dramatic monologues. "Faith" not only is one of the more appealing voices I discovered, but also she embodies the same peculiar mixture of sacred and profane that I came to love as a preacher's kid. Moreover, something in her character immediately resonated with my wife, which makes her a favorite of both of us.

Since my thirties, I've gotten progressively more un-churched and yet my spiritual life has deepened because of poetry. W.S. Merwin, who is also a preacher's son, once said, "All poetry begins with listening and ends with hearing something." I believe that as well. And what I have come to hear is, as Keats put it, "the holiness of the heart's affections and the truth of the imagination." "The Visitation" and "Durable Goods" were selected from my recent work because they reflect this credo from Keats. The first attests to the sweet ache of heaven that dwells in us when our earthly love is forced to change. And the latter speaks to what endures in spite of the changes.

▲ ▲ ▼ ▲ ▲

Curtis Derrick lives with his wife and daughter in Columbia, where he teaches at Midlands Technical College. Since 1989, he has also taught for the Johns Hopkins University's Center for Talented Youth (CTY), for which he designed the poetry tutorial. Through CTY's Distance Education Program, he has mentored young poets from across the continental United States, as well as Hong Kong, Korea, Jordan, and Sweden. His work has appeared in numerous small magazines and has been recognized by the South Carolina Fiction Project. He has received an AWP Intro Award and the poetry fellowship from the South Carolina Academy of Authors. He holds an MFA in creative writing from Warren Wilson College.

# SONNET

How dare someone to say aloud that God
Is dead, that He no longer lingers here—
The Father who has given us this sod
And still preserves these things that are most dear!

I wish the men who say that God has died
Would take a look above and all around—
The birds, the trees, the air, the mountainside,
The sun, and all the glories that abound.

Our Lord has given us these very things
That we take so for granted day by day,
Though He, Almighty God, hears mutterings
Of foolish men, who scoff instead of pray.

God is not dead, for it is by his grace
That we are standing here upon this place.

*1966*

# GUSTA

She taught us painting in the park;
Setting up easels in the grass or on brick sidewalks:
Massive oak trees sun-washed and sprawling,
With stoles of Spanish moss draped from every limb,

Or wrought-iron stoops, mostly curved ascensions
With marble stairs,
That worked like Jacob's ladder
To heavenly parlors of old Savannah.

I had no talent, crude technique,
And lacked a sense of color.
But her brown teeth grinned
At everything I did. She glowed

When she smiled, and flaunted every line
Life had wreaked across her face, cigarette
Dangling from her lips as she spoke,
Sometimes cursing. Her obscenities like candy

To the adolescent ear. Hearing her husky voice
Rasp the afternoon when her Renault Dauphin
Once more sputtered to a halt in traffic,
The world was wild with promise,

So we laughed, pushing her to the curb,
This woman, unlike our mothers, divorced,
Childless, and willing to take us in on Tuesdays,
Steering us by the hand towards something beautiful.

*1974*

# FAITH NEIGHBORS, PREACHER'S DAUGHTER

I see you, Dewey Brazelton, watching
my tits bounce as I dance, filled
with the Holy Ghost, anointed,
sweaty from my religious act, as I speak
in the secret tongues and swing these two
serpents, big as oak-root, writhing stiffly.
Tomorrow you'll visit me at the K-Mart. Grinning,
and running your hands through my lingerie counter,
you'll ask if I try on the panties and negligees,
and then sniff a few like a dog on point.
I see you, Dewey Brazelton; watching me,
getting moist all in your crotch where it protrudes,
and I wonder     I wonder if the Lord God Almighty'd
smite me where I stand for aiming these vipers
right at yours as it hides inside that seersucker suit.

*1984*

## THE VISITATION

Unbridled, immodest mirth!
Stripping for her bath, my daughter
flings garments off along her path,
barely pausing as she sprints.
A manic munchkin,
bee-like, buzzing me.
"Come back! my little moon."

The midget wobble in her cheeks,
tan-lined from the beach,
accelerates. I take the bait.
Yet suddenly these hands
that cupped her bottom,
steering her infant sleep
from room to room, now brake.
Her fleeing grin is different—
with a glinting eye—a trailing lure,
rehearsing for a groom. Full tilt,
she vanishes out of reach.

Around the corner,
down the dim corridor,
her backlit silhouette chirps
from the bathroom door,
"You can't catch me,
Daddy." Then—slam!

I listen, stranded in the dark.
No deadbolt
to lodge inside the jamb this time—
a lesson learned. I linger to see
the water stops, thankful when it does.

Inside, her chatter's brimming over—a love song
to the light she's in (and is). As if by summons,
my dead father draws closer as I listen.
His ear is pressed inside my heart to hear

the granddaughter he never knew.
So luminous this tinge of darkness is,
his old laugh comes flooding back
the way I remember, whenever
he was visited
by unexpected joy.

*1998*

# DURABLE GOODS

A child has smothered at the county dump.
Old refrigerator—Hotpoint, the paper said,
exhumed by rain. Quoted were the boy's twin
with other kin, latched tight with grief. So flimsy
is our design. Our quivering pump of heart
breaks too many ways—from sorrows, fears, or joys,
real or not. One night our Honda Odyssey

went off a bridge. All perished save for me. Jarred,
I woke from the horror, went from room to room
to check. Kissing heads, tears welled up. Reality
suddenly too sweet for dreams. Jostled,
my wife surfaced from her sleep with no idea
the need I held her with. We drifted off
like spiral galaxies, spooned in the clock's glow.

Once upon a time, time's face at night stood still,
a quiet phosphorescence. Now, luminescent
liquid crystals clock our passing, the glowing
tabulations of our lives in the pop-bead world
of molecules. Years hence, one half-life at a time,
the stardust atoms in our bones—carbon, calcium,
iron—will break free, grounded in the darkness

of earth. Skulls, ribs, femurs absorbed into heaven—
the hereafter, invisible, but here now beneath our feet.
And we would disappear like whispers dissolved
in the night air, except the poetry of earth is never dead.
And words, recounted, are heard like these—a wife:
"What's the matter?"—her husband: "I dreamt you drowned
without me." In every language, words open eyes and fly,

like the cawing crows in the dawn I'm sitting in,
with Virgil's words now open on my lap: Optima dies
prima fugit: the best days are the first to flee.
And in this high summer in Carolina, mimosas
scent the humidity, where someone's child has died
at the county dump, and a jet's contrail scores
the sky, turns to wisps, and leaves no scar.

*2002*

# LINDA ANNAS FERGUSON
## Poetry Fellow, 2004

Sometimes I feel as if I am a detached observer of myself. I am me watching the other me, the writer. In the beginning, I think the words are about my life or something I observed, but then as I scribble more, I realize there is a part of the poem that is more than I am.

The poem becomes a hole, which has nothing and everything. The gift that it gives me is a connection to the rest of the world. Pausing at its edge is not a passive act. The darker the hole, and the more slippery its rim, the closer I stand to my true self.

The hole is very old and wise. I offer it my lonely things, my angers, my claims, confessions, a memory of Mother's hand on my hot forehead—hoping that something from its strange depths will talk back to me.

Other times the hole is filled with water. Its surface becomes a mirror. When I write about my father, long dead, I see *me*. When I read about him out loud to others, they tell me they see their own father. Another time at another reading, *we* are the mirror. The life that was a father's sees itself in us, in the words we didn't write or say, in the baby lost, the love found, in the times we didn't go, the times we wanted to stay.

My job is to find out what the hole is trying to be, what shape it is to take. I listen, lower my ideas down into its darkness to see what happens, sometimes settling for the soft truth, hoping it might be enough. It doesn't have a bottom. I often imagine it does, just to be able to believe I am finished, to linger over a poem's closing line. I want a bottom! I want a bottom with resolve and clarity, a bottom that in the end will somehow make the words better than they are.

Writing poetry is a solitary work in which I reveal all my best-kept secrets. It demands I be truthful, if not to the facts, to the poem itself, or it won't be any good. I read a newly written verse out loud to myself over and over, then sometimes muse at how I spend most of my life searching for a synonym, the exact noun, the perfect sound.

Other times I am silent, reluctant to share my joys and regrets with others, as if we were all separate from one another, as if the words weren't good enough, as if holding on were giving. In the end I feed them, page by page, to the hole because I want to see more than myself in the mirror; because I can never explain the hole—because as long as I live there will always be a hole.

▲ ▲ ▼ ▲ ▲

Linda Annas Ferguson lives in Charleston where she served as the 2003-2004 poet-in-residence for the Gibbes Museum of Art. She was the 2002 winner of the Palanquin Press Competition of the University of South Carolina-Aiken for her chapbook, *It's Hard to Hate a Broken Thing*. Her second chapbook, *Last Chance to Be Lost*, was the 2003 winner of the Kentucky Writers' Coalition Poetry Competition. A former winner of the Poetry Fellowship of the South Carolina Academy of Authors, she was also a 2003 finalist in the John Ciardi Book Prize in Poetry of Bookmark Press of the University of Missouri, Kansas City.

## ADOPTED, AGE FIVE

My new mother has left me
waiting on the stoop
to go inside to buy clothes
I don't want.

This is a day when everything is wrong.
I think of a far away bed,
a pillow with just the right softness,
my real mother who gave me away

how I fit into the folds of her skirt
when the strangers came,
chewed its hem as I had done before
when she didn't mind,

think of my older brother, almost fifteen,
coming home from school to find me gone,
toys left by a door, except for the small
unworried doll in my hand,

think of my mother's eyes,
distant as the day my father died,
how they stared past me
as if I weren't there.

The door of the store swings open.
arms rustling with paper packages
wrap around me, lift my pliable bones,
hold me close,

this soft, larger body stealing mine.

*2000*

## Cotton Mill Hill

The graveyard shift gravitates
down the hill toward fragments
of light in the distance, windows
rise in salutation from the dark earth.

Departing voices rasp in thin dispersion.
My father begins the long walk home.
Parasites of cotton cling to his clothes.
He wears them like a second skin.

His eyes grow accustomed
to the lack of light near the church.
He remembers grave robbers he surprised
last May, bones thrown about in the grass.

It had taken him hours
to return the dead
to the dignity they deserved,
restore the integrity of the turf.

The family never knew.

He had felt the lack and want
in the discarded gravedigger's shovel
as he gave back soil
to the cheated earth.

Later this morning, warm in his own bed,
he will hoard his four hours
deep in the fermented smell of sleep,
cotton sheet stretched over his head.

In the evening,
he has a field to plow under.

*1999*

# THE FOURTH FLOOR

While you are dying in ICU
the waiting room is alive
with the noise of cartoons,
Elmer Fudd shooting the rascally rabbit,
the road runner's awaited beep
before the coyote's demise,
Gumby's stretch into strange shapes.

Every four hours I am allowed to visit
your distorted body, watch the respirator
animate your lungs, listen to the bleep
of monitors measure time,
the silence of a single IV feeding you
one more hour of your pretend life.

*2002*

# My Mother Doesn't Know Me

To her, I'm the mild-mannered woman
who cooks her meals.
She is going to leave me a tip
when she finds her purse.

She sits for hours, eyebrow
cocked in a wrinkled study
as if she could fathom
the distance between us,

saves pieces of thread
in a coffee can,
picked from her afghan all day
while both our lives unravel.

Thanksgiving, she put a hammer
in the oven at 400 degrees,
spent the rest of the day
on the back porch step,

wanting only to leave
this strange house,
silently wringing her hands
as if her body could not contain her.

*2003*

# THE QUESTION

Have you ever wanted to go back,
live life in reverse, watch
how a butterfly folds itself
into the cocoon, how the wet-winged
fledgling pulls the egg around itself,
seals broken edges,

feel yourself reenter the womb,
take a held breath, ride
the phoenix down into fire,
reclaim the flame of your innocence,
the red and gold ember of desire,

write your name with a hot coal
on the imperfect slate of possibility,
where everything you will ever love
already exists complete and whole?

*2001*

# STARKEY FLYTHE
**Poetry Fellow, 1986**

These poems have to do with image, or the more modern image, advertisement, pictures that stick, or sell.

Politicians, presidents, parties, churches, companies spend huge amounts—your money, usually—investigating how we respond to what they say, do, wear, where they live, their families, friends, breeds of dogs.

PR people and psychologists have discovered the superficial is as important to an image as anything more profound. An American flag in the lapel softens stories of draft dodging. Kissing a baby erases tales of premarital goings-on.

Early Christians told their stories in mosaics and fresco cycles. Rulers inserted their own heads, donors, your money again near the toes of the venerated, often becoming saints themselves if the images sold and stuck.

Poetry, perhaps more than other art forms, reveals how little changes in the world. Time stands still to the persistent heartbeat of image and meter. Mothers nurse babies, their hearts banging together. Mary Magdalene (Madonna, now) sports her long, golden hair and the past that accompanies such tresses. We, the watchers, the admirers, the would-bes, want to be good, to be like, alas, to be powerful, discovered, permanented. Somebody. And yet, we want to believe, too, and still be ourselves.

St. Francis strips—poverty—his wealth goes to the church, we are admonished to give—obedience—to give all—love—and in love sufficient quantities, denial, becomes the other admonition, chastity.

Sophia Loren feeds the world with her ample cleavage—and Jayne, who would do the same, or anything for that matter, never quite rises above the level of camp because the artists who made Sophia and Theodosia, Justinian's Christian wife, daughter of an animal trainer, once an actress, then a prostitute, then a Christian empress, the mosaic, and, say, St. Catherine—her mystical marriage—could not find the raw material in Jayne, or the resulting pay-out to achieve that kind of royal, religious endurance, though Sophia's sister was married to the son of Mussolini, the jack-booted image, and Jayne was married to Mr. World, or Mr. Universe, the Atlas of his day. Those who made Marilyn or Elvis or Diana knew how to make the image last. Jayne's handlers missed. And Cher? Only time will tell, though what a boost Sonny's running into a tree on the ski slopes gives the story.

So the funny and the sad march together sometimes in poetry, and what we remember survives as story, sometimes, as joke—St. Peter says to the rabbi, the Baptist minister and the nun—and for a moment we forget death, inevitability. Why we/they are at the Gate. Why we are writing about them, why we are trying to remember.

The picture is there. Not just a one-instrument piece. The whole vision thing. Copied at the Xerox machine. Repeated, collated. Office workers have mooned the machine. Hamlet, entire, is copied in a few strokes. Genius is a push button. Cher runs into Diana (of the Ephesians), Diana of the Ephesians, a fertility doll, her chest covered with bull testicles, runs into Diana (of the Spencers), her husband's face, or hers, covered with egg. So it goes.

Finally, to heaven, the actual place of our dreams, not Hollywood. "You like that one?" Grandma Moses says to Dwight Eisenhower, a painter, too, when his party sends him out to pick up some old votes. "This one?" said Grandma, "I'll add anything you like, clothesline, cat, snow, Christmas tree? Or take it out?" So much for primitive image, the staring saint, the broken cross. So much for the singularity of art. So drawn we could enjoy a Sistine Chapel ceiling in every mobile home in South Carolina. In the proper hands, Grandma Moses could've made a Jayne. A Marilyn. Hear the rumors flying— Grandma and Ike. See the picture, his short jacket—home made—D. Day— the two of them in image's landscape, painting. Little people—poets—tying to get at them, trying to hack out an image and get into the picture. Lilliputians storming Easter Island.

▲ ▲ ▼ ▲ ▲

Starkey Flythe served with the U.S. Army in East Africa, has taught in public schools and state colleges, and in the Governor's School for the Arts and Humanities summer programs. He has two books of poems, *They Say Dancing*, and, *Paying the Anesthesiologist*, from Furman University's Ninety-Six Press, stories anthologized in the *Best American*, *O. Henry*, and *New Stories from the South*, annuals, and a collection of stories, *Lent: The Slow Fast*, University of Iowa Press. He lives in North Augusta.

# CHER

I'm lying on the floor with Cher.  Her
stomach's as flat as an envelope
an hour after the paycheck's been spent.
"Do you exercise?" I ask trying hard
and failing to think questions
nobody else has, trying to write,
do sit-ups the same time.  She could be
a wonder of the ancient world,
not the pyramids or the hanging gardens,
though these triangles, these tendrils have been
emphasized in her make up, her publicity, Diana, Diana
of the Ephesians, the temple itself, her hair
black as squid spit, the woman on the raisin
box, Sunmaid, raisins growing, a child, I
thought, out of her head, Diana, the idol
Paul railed against, preaching the unseen
God who would put Ephesus out of business,
the hundred-breasted dolls, fertility toys
Ephesus peddled all over the eastern Med,
only now, archeologists say, they're not
breasts, bulls' balls, though the idea's the same,
I guess. The harbor at Ephesus is stilted over,
ruined by cutting the timber on the hillsides,
the oaks felled in the sacred groves as every country
is ruined, not by love, Paul, by erosion,
the ships built to bring back something new
we wear now, burn, war over later, worship
as the object disappears.  Paul,
you're to blame, they say, for the wrong turn
Christianity took.  Should I tell Cher this?  She
probably knows, could buy Ephesus, dredge the harbor
bottom.  Cher could do anything.  Look great in a glass
dress, her fundament tattooed with a spider,
the web of young men, rich world of single names
tying up her motions in perfect freedom.  Paul
can't touch her.  I fill pad after pad.
She tells me her nose has been fixed,
that she never sounded Bronxy before they narrowed it,
through she's from there, or near.  She
worries her baby, Chastity's, not a baby
anymore.  Chas for short.  I'm not sure

I'll be able to get up off the floor.  Not Cher.
She flies to the phone, room service, orders
a drink, anything, she says, with an umbrella in it.
The pyramids are inverted in the exercise mat.
The green columns from Diana's temple went
to build Constantines' Christian church,
now and then a mosque, a museum.  No matter
what you preach, Paul, the forest is cut,
the stones used again.  Cher smiles.  Not at me.  Beyond.

*1988*

## ST. FRANCIS RENOUNCES HIS EARTHLY FATHER

Yes, everything, his clothes ripped off
in the front hall, everything, socks,
underdrawers, a sort of  T-shirt
chemise thing men wore back then,
his shoes—when you lose your shoes
you have to step on it, in it,
sometimes, his cloak a retainer
has his hands on already—people
were always fighting over cloaks—
the Crucifixion—God knows
overcoats are never cheap,
so much material, wool, big
buttons.


     His father's in despair,
his only son, only child.  He
remembers when he was born,
the masses of thanksgiving, a boy!
The little white cakes—cigars weren't
invented—they handed out
in the streets.  He gave his employees
the day off, the week.  A son!
The name would live, the family.
Now he's walking out the door.  Naked.
The household who've loved him from a baby,
wept him through the plague
that hollowed the city,
huddle dumbstruck around the scene.
You can never hide anything,
thinks the father bitterly,
from servants.

          Francis looks back,
the house, his room, the pantry,
stores brimming with excess.
He takes one last breath, one deep
breath, can almost recite dinner.
The church across the street holds up
a thin paper of bread, rings
its cacophonous bells.

"When you lose
everything," warns the father,
"you need everything."  "More," whispers
the wily steward, his hands penning
a new will.  "When you lose
everything" Francis tries to say,
his eyes tearing from the wind,
"You find everything," but he can't
quite get it out, something gnawing
in his stomach, the memory of birds,
roasting on the spit, olive oil
dripping into the fire, pigs fat as clouds,
lambs bristling with rosemary, the wine
red as blood they said was shed
for him, would never cease to flow.

*2002*

# SOPHIA LOREN EYEING JAYNE MANSFIELD'S BOSOM

Curiosity or condemnation? Of course neither
has touched her roll, certainly not the butter.
Not here to eat but be eaten by every eye.
Premiere, film fest, some award, charity
(which began at home) wondering all day
what to put on, how far to go, or stay
in—or out—of a dress. Who could believe science—
silicone, rhinoplasty, peroxide—the alliance
of hope and pain had anything to do with such
Èclairs, custard oozing every nubile niche?
Jayne—do you not love the spelling of her nayme?—
will be decapitated, or was it cut in twayne?—
read *Hollywood Babylon*—in a car accident;
Sophia marry a man old enough to be her parent,
short enough to be the child she'll have trouble conceiving.
Imagine that boy's joy feeding, cleaving
Matterhorn and Everest, only to be superseded
by brother Paolo? Edguardo? Cesare? (Hail Caesar!)
The camera loved these women. I did, too.
Sophia could act, Jayne would've learned to,
given time. Which won't be given. Time hates
beauty. Sophia hawks eyeglass frames, now, silverplate,
tortoise shell: at Forest Lawn, Jayne and worms fellate.

*1995*

# HEAVEN

In the world to come, it will always be
morning, somewhere between breakfast cooking
and snow, and still time to stretch against clean
sheets, clean every night, our bed made ever new,
love reaching back, the children angels but well,
asleep in another room, their own dreams.

Outside, the wind will blow peach-blossom petals.
We will know everything and forget it.
The house will be paid for and all our needs,
yet thirst and desire will keep a place: wars
no more, though reasonable argument; words
will fail but kisses complete, the spring eternal
with weather, storms, solstices every day
and summer still to urge the garden.  Then will be now,
tomorrow closer, today farther away.

God will reveal himself a soft, speechless hand
to hold us, rub us, as he would love
from looking-glass, or greed from gold.
it won't care whether we go on Sunday,
Monday will serve as well, and never any wash.
He won't blame us for our cross beginnings,
or remind us of the end, put off now forever.
All will be sky, clear and weightless and blue.

It is so wonderful I could go on.
But first we must turn away, wink at the dust
that catches in the corners, fills our breaths,
and cry for the beauty we cannot explain,
so pale and purposeless we are told, so rich
we know, so much like the spotless world to come.

*1982*

## THEY TOLD ME

you were dead, people are always
talking, implication everything—
what you died of and how—AIDS,
plaque, smoke—death as consequence,
shock and surprise nothing.  So why
should your ghost appear next to me
at the Xerox (Greek for shadow)—
Hamlet, Sr. copying, copying,
Remember!  You couldn't
stop talking, the single man
who lives alone, your mother's burial,
how Jews do, inter the day,
monument a year later.  I heard
every word—when the dead speak—
nota bene—the arrow shifts left,
back space unraveling every touch.

Office Max—computers smalling all
we know—Newton, Jesus,
Leonardo, insecticized. You aren't
dead, appear exact, no ghost, quoting
Mark Twain—"Reports of my death…"
used books, what else in anyone?
Go, live down your reputation.  Clear,
(the green button) unpaid bills
dunning the life you spent, run,
before the paper tops the trees.
How to tell those who told me?
They gave me your death, a gift; I
withhold your life, the antidote.
How many others don't know?
We should make sure before we say
but that this world should be silent.

*2003*

# ANGELA KELLY
## Poetry Fellow, 2000

When I was a child, my favorite story was "Goldilocks and The Three Bears." There were distinct reasons for this: I had gold locks and my favorite playmates were bears, albeit stuffed teddy bears. I was a lonely child, deliberately so, and I regarded other children with suspicion. Adults had mystery and secrets and power. Children did not. And when they arrived at my house, they bustled with a disturbing energy and tended to take over my most prized possessions without warning. A story with beloved bears was, therefore, a good refuge. But I hated the ending. My mother was forced to redesign the ending each evening when she read me the story. Goldilocks was not allowed to jump out the window and escape when the bears came home. In my version of the story, she was captured and eaten. After all, she broke in their house, ate their porridge, broke their good chairs and slept uninvited in their beds. *She deserved to be eaten.*

And in my mind, I deserved to rewrite the endings to whatever story I heard. Whatever did not strike me as just or sufficiently interesting could be reinterpreted. I was not only editor, but judge, jury and executioner. This is when you know you are a poet. When you give in to your own natural tendency to deconstruct, reconstruct, polish, embellish and generally impose your own version of reality. To manipulate a situation of interest with sheer language. It is one of the complexities and joys of poetry to be able to give credence to what you like or remake whatever interests you by simply putting words on a page in an order designed to please only you, the poet. If it's done well, it will hopefully please others. Your words will convey universal meaning and give a sense of shared humanity to the reader.

The other aspect of being a poet, of realizing yourself as an artist, is the ability to intensely examine the everyday. Intent observation of the moment and acknowledgment of the particular. It does not matter if you are a philanthropist in a penthouse or a peach farmer of the Piedmont, if you drive a dump truck or sit in a factory counting widgets—you should intensely examine all around you. It is dear, precious, unique. Dirt or skyscrapers. Sweet fruit in an orchard or an old woman with arthritic hands from years on the production line. The life you live is the well of water from which you must draw. The place you occupy and how you occupy it is where the art comes from. Bring intensity and acute observation to the forefront of your life and the words, the art will emerge. And if there are bears or little girls who scarf all the porridge, then let it be so. Or not.

▲ ▲ ▼ ▲ ▲

Angela Kelly is the 2003 winner of the Yemassee Poetry Prize and received the Emerging Voices Award from the Southern Women Writers Conference. Her chapbook, *Weighing the body back down*, was the winner of the 1996 Tennessee Prize from Middle Tennessee State University. She has received fellowships from the Vermont Studio Center and the Virginia Center for the Creative Arts. Angela is a graduate of the University of South Carolina Spartanburg.

# THE BOOK THE DEVIL'S CHAPLAIN MIGHT WRITE

*"What a book the devil's chaplain might write*
*on the clumsy, wasteful, blundering, low*
*and horribly cruel works of nature!"*
— Charles Darwin

The monkey, the organ grinder.
This is his third monkey
each one different
the first, a charmer
the second, a dreamer
and now this one—praedominari.

This one who throws his braided cap
to the greedy-never-give-back audience,
this one who urinates on the children,
this one, a scrawny son of a bitch,
the gilded vest hanging from his ribs
worse than the hair shirt of Christ.

The organ grinder is a hump-back.
Curved to his shoulder, the cumbersome cross
of accordion, heavy as the stone
one should roll away so that Lazarus
might come forth, dazed, blinking
at pale sunrise, owning up to the myth.

For this one, there is no resurrection,
only Darwin with his inexplicable stew
of lizards and birds, then beasts and mammals.
But in the wagon, it is still the monkey, the ape,
who runs his dark, tapered fingers tender along
the old man's skull, among the thin strands

of silver hair, some lice, dandruff, an occasional
scab and the monkey is munching, calm, content.
There is no accordion yaw, no giddy tinkling,
no music at all as the old man sleeps.  Just as on
that sixth final night when God made the circus,
Ferris wheel and carnival.   And the monkey sang.

*1999*

# FEAR COMES LIKE A WHISTLE, A DEPOT, THE TRAIN ITSELF

*Jesus done left Chicago* (old blues song)

After years of no Jesus, he looks at me now
he's a metal head, a reflection off the examining light,
which aims heated breath along my goose-bump thighs.

His disciple, the doctor, wields his spectrum,
a locomotive of pain whistles through my tunnel.
Down the hall to another station.

The bored nurse now bustles and brims.
Past doors with yellow charts, women
shivering in paper gowns. Ultrasound Three.

A black baseball has been pitched to my uterus.
Healthy fetuses from gestation posters watch the doctor
measure my baseball—diameter—circumference—

Left behind, the latest issue of Cosmo advises me
    "The Secret Parts of Your Body Which He Really Wants."
Womb full of black baseballs is not on the list.

I strip the paper robe from my shoulders,
skin the color of a clam pried open,
breasts cold as buckets of November sand.

I put on a skirt I shall never wear again.
Nod as they move my name up and up
on the surgery roster. Tomorrow.

Then out on the avenue blinking, chiming,
like a pinball I ricochet from lamppost to door,
    from block to block, store to store.

Each person I pass looks happy, healthy, whole,
I want to beat them, to hold them tender as egg yolk,
whisper to them how their true and careful bodies

will hide hatchets and hurricanes,
windmills and cactus, oil spills and dregs,
    all those hobo miles of cold steel rail.

*2000*

# SHOULD BECKETT WRITE *THE ESSAY OF THE DIVORCEÉ*

The debacle of her life now:
Wasps, white bellied in the window sills,
Frozen entrees: chicken pot pie, meat loaf for one.
Sunflowers which crumble against the unused shed,
Puppies without distemper shots, no leash.

Nights when the yearnings are benevolent.
Mornings when the car battery is dead and bullets beckon.
The Church is now polite.
The young man in Accounting loses interest
Perhaps a woman with real hips is unaccountable.

In *Waiting for Godot*, there were two and
A donkey, of sorts, which was often whipped,
There on a stark stage, under a dead tree.
Vladimir had all the great lines:

    "It's too much for one man."
    "No one ever suffers but you.  I don't count."
    "Hmm.  It'd give us an erection…with all that follows."
    "Did I ever leave you?"

Despite the stage, despite every low-rate,
Bad opening night, she still believes in
Yes, the tragicomedy in two acts.

In a man, the post-coital nights when
He's standing in his pale boxers,
Spent and rosy, opening the fridge,
Hopeful of roast beef, good mustard, cold beer.

*1998*

# AFTER TOO MUCH WINE

My mother tells me that she and my father no longer make love.
A marriage forty-three years and the loving stops.  She is crying,
the dog growing anxious and I can think of nothing to say.

The doctors say it is medical.  They propose this drug, that drug
but one is bad for heart patients, others scratched in the name
of prostate and asthma.  They propose some therapies,
    "alternate ways of pleasure."
My father snorts.  Walks away from one doctor and another.
My mother says "sorry" as she closes the doors.
She looks in the mirror, sees a body dumpling soft,
webbed with the fine scritchings of sixty years.
    Beauty has stormed off like a house guest, insulted,
slamming the door, something precious falling from a shelf.

My father does not hear the door slam,
has no tuck  for house guests, is always suspicious
of beauty for beauty's sake.  In the name of love,
the best he can do is say
"good pot roast."
Hunched over his TV tray he's watching the detectives
who solve everything in sixty sweet minutes.
Beside him, the dog begs a morsel, his table scrap love.

    During the long evening, they both cuddle the dog,
pet the dog, talk their secret language to the dog, who divides
himself equally between them,  loving them fiercely with
every hair of his body and each night, getting into bed,
they call the dog in, for he sleeps between them,
a bucket of blonde fur and furious blood,
    who'll twitch through the night with dreams of the chase.

1997

# In The Kitchen

That evening when I diced myself to ribbons
among the Vidalia onions, red peppers,
bella mushrooms, my fingers, adorned
with your rings for these many years,
took a long time to bleed or beg

for scant attention as you sat on the barstool,
noodling a bottle of beer, complaining subtly
of a woman you work with, voluptuous,
red-headed,   I had met her   here and there.
Knowing your desires I could track it each day,

slowly, mentally (but nothing more) you were unfaithful.
Your hands parting my thighs were yet your hands
plucking shy at the hem of her skirt.
A penniless child of the street, brave enough to
eye-ball the closed door to the candy shoppe,

to dream of whips of licorice, cherries in chocolate.
So perhaps I placed the blade there myself,
sliced along the bone, admired the jet of crimson
bright against julienned vegetables.   Suddenly you
were everywhere, a warm tourniquet of salve and gauze.

Later, an inch of salt, a dish of hot water
in which to whirl away stiffness and pain.
How tenderly you held the wilted flower of my wrist,
your own eyes squinched in communal pain,
then our midnight smiles of suture, of being, once again, one.

*2001*

# JOHN LANE
**Poetry Fellow, 1985**

I t's been twenty years since I won the South Carolina Arts Commission's Individual Arts Fellowship in Poetry. That year I had just turned thirty. I had no career outside of writing. I was poor, independent, living the dangerous dreams first articulated by Dylan Thomas, Ezra Pound, and Kenneth Rexroth. Art was my focus and remaining clearly outside the dominant culture was my quest. My ambition was to write poems, and the Commission's $5,000 gave me time and encouragement to do so. Thank God for big government! Now I'm a college professor and my career for almost twenty years has been that of a teacher within which I have somehow continued to write. I have produced as much prose as poetry in the past fifteen or so years, something I couldn't have anticipated back when I saw poetry, as James Dickey once put it, as the true center of my creative wheel.

The five poems I've included here span thirty years. They are in chronological order. This sort of thing has come to mean more to me now that I'm old enough to become historic to myself. The first was written when I was twenty-two and the last, several years ago. "Waking in the Blue Ridge" was composed when I was still a student at Wofford College in the mid-'70s. It's one of those poems that got me labeled as a "nature writer" and I still enjoy reciting it. The long narrative "Returning Home, Saxon Mills" was one of the first poems I wrote trying to deal with my own complex personal history as the son of a mill worker. "The Small Losses" is a love poem with elements of landscape meditation. "Sweet Tea" has become one of my greatest hits, requested almost everywhere I go to read. I wrote it when I got tired of trying to explain to Yankee audiences what it means to be Southern. I once got a standing ovation reading it at the South Carolina Book Festival in the late '90s when I intoned the lines, "Take the damn flag off/ the state capitol. It doesn't mean anything to me./But leave me my sweet tea, a recipe for being civil." "My Dead Father on Vacation" is one of a sequence of poems written in the 1990s that imagine my dead father back to life. In this one I take him to Myrtle Beach, a fine place to take a man dead almost fifty years.

The poet Gregory Orr talks of "the thread of poetry" in his memoir, *The Blessing*. He believes a life lived from poem-to-poem can bless us, save us even. Poetry can bring order from chaos. It can create for us a map to live by, an emotional landscape to inhabit. Looking back at these five poems I see a map, and not surprising to those who know me, there is a river running through it. There's a flowing, an emptying out, some serious gradient, and a grave motion toward meaning. Enjoy the float.

▲ ▲ ▼ ▲ ▲

John Lane's poetry has appeared in numerous collections (*Quarries*, *Body Poems*, *As the World Around Us Sleeps*, *Against Information & Other Poems*, and *The Dead Father Poems*) and his personal essays in *Weed Time*, *Waist Deep in Black Water* and most recently, the book-length narrative, *Chattooga*. He has edited anthologies and conducted workshops and readings all across the United States. One of the three founders of the Hub City Writers Project, Lane is currently associate professor of English and creative writing at Wofford College in Spartanburg, South Carolina.

## WAKING IN THE BLUE RIDGE

In the animal light of early morning
dreams persist but I am quickly
victim to the world's precision—

how oaks become one
in a web of blue above,
and the fox bursts
toward the nested quail,
or in tricks of color
copperheads coil
where they could not be.

All this in the hour
before breakfast, in the heaven
of unnoticed verdancy and light.

*1977*

# Returning Home, Saxon Mills

I walk red roads, unpaved, blowing away,
kicking leeched-dry clay. August.
Near a lake fenced with chain link,
red brick walls of the cotton mill shine
in mid-morning Southern sun.
Mama says I was born with cotton dust
in my chest. I cough once for her, once
for all my aunts and uncles.
Mama quit school at 16 to work this mill.

"Boy, you know the hum of a spinning room,
the clack of the looms.
You know it deep in your bones."

Now in the quiet of my 24th year, I hear
the hum of the mill, and her humming
the numb walk home after a shift change.
When she wakes in mid-afternoon it is 1945
and her life begins again
to stretch awake, move out into the world.
The biscuits and gravy are still there,
and the Luckies, and the soldiers on the streets
from Camp Croft, all glad the war ended.
The soldier who took her away
from the lint and heat leans on the mill gate
waiting for her. It is October, he holds
a cigarette from the wind.

This same soldier will leave her in a year.
Then she'll leave to go to Florida, to find
her family, working people, forever poor,
ready to move, carrying her clothes,
my unborn sister,
nothing left of marriage but the cheap ring.

There was her father, Lonnie, the house painter,
in Lantana. Lonnie, always drinking,
laughing at poverty. Then he was lucky.
He was always lucky. He bought good cheap land,
sold it for a quick profit, a bottle,
and a fast car—headed north.

He left their world, returned years later
as a farmer in North Carolina.
In ten years he was crying, when dying of cancer,
he saw my mama, his daughter, then in her own
frame house, coming to visit a last time.
His only life bloomed in the faces of children.

There was her mama, Hulda, with breasts
hanging like sacks, who only got fatter,
sat in a wicker chair, lived like a vine
growing outward through children.
She made biscuits for breakfast,
kneaded the dough with fat hands,
washed clothes of six kids and a grandchild
in a wringer, dried on a line under Florida sun.
The old clothes hung stiff with the heat, many sizes,
the shed skins of seven growing children.

Then mama woke in the Florida heat and it was 1952.
She caught the train north with my sister,
worked mills in the beginning of another war.
She met a man, a wanderer, who would be my father.
They married, something grew, a family and a business
pumping as on the main highway.

In photos I've seen my father  brooding—
a face stretched tight over some loss in him,
his mind working, like tonguing a hole in a tooth.
In November, the trees stiff with frost, mama
found him dead, as the running car, hose from exhaust
shook off the cold in our driveway.

Once, when I was five, my sister twelve,
in our first rented house in Spartanburg,
the three of us watched the moon circle down.
Mama sang a song to us often:

"See the Man in the Moon.
Mama gonna come back soon.
But don't you worry none.
She won't drink no more bad whiskey."

Now in the August heat, it's shift change.
The whistle hangs in the stiff air.
The lake stirs a moment, then is quiet.
People slip like shadows into the last
of the soft morning sun.
A man cracks his knuckles as he leaves,
another checks his head to be sure
of the billed cap
he will plow in this evening.

And I see all my uncles in the shadows—
Tommy, Norman, and the twins, Bobby and Billy,
still young and slim.
This for me is another time, but nothing changes.
The war is over, but which war?
Only now, the machines are not so loud.
Only now, the windows are bricked shut.
Then, in the last shadows, as the people thin,
I see a dark woman humming.
It could be 1945, or it could be today.
She's headed home,
humming some songs she thinks I wouldn't know.

*1980*

# THE SMALL LOSSES

I wanted to speak for all
the small losses between us,
to warm the space around
our separated silences
with some simple luminous clarity.
Once I said the word *skunk* and saw
your face warm to a place, a particular
night when you lost all bearing
and swerved past the black and white
elegance caught in your killing lights.
Or the time you did not miss
and the stiff spice of skunk
sat in the car for nearly a week
like some other body separating us.

I am reminded of a field we saw
where a thousand scattered flecks
of black took to the air.
*Birds*, you said, *thousands*.
My mind rushed through every name.
*Starlings*, I said, *grackles*,
*finches, wrens, crows*.
I tried them all, each
with a hope of some surety.
Then something in that selfish
dance of naming left a cold field
between us.  The birds
had left before we caught
much more than a spray
of black to carry with us.
That night you said *thousands*
and my mind searched a winter
field for something lost.

But this morning I listen
to you in the kitchen rolling
out dough, pounding the greasy lump
between palms brown with flour.

You are making our bread,
you are measuring our lives,

pressing them into loaves.

The rhythmic pounding is a song
you want to keep from me:

*This is the flour of mornings together.*
*This, the milk of longing.*
*This, the perfect egg you said we'd make*
*between us in darkness.*
*And my hands like sledges of winter ice*
*break down the meaning*
*of separate longings and work*
*it to make all one.*

Out my window I watch a small
finch pinch berries off cedars.
I trace its gray flick in and out
of shadows in branches.
This morning it should be quieted
from its animal freedom,
it should be caged,
there should be hunts and stews.

*1980*

## Sweet Tea

God rested on the seventh day, but early in the morning,
    before the sun strained into the Southern sky,
    she made sweet tea from scratch.  She boiled the water
    in a black kettle, put in the orange pekoe bags
    and let them stand as the water perked, and then
    she did what gods know to do: she heaped in Dixie
    Crystal sugar while the brew was still warm as the day.

For God so loved the world she made sweet tea.  For she served
    the tea to anyone who admired her creation.  To anyone
    walking down the street of the wet new neighborhood,
    to the mailman delivering early on that next day
    of that second week, to the milkman in his truck, the black
    man working in the yard, to the white man selling peaches
    door-to-door.  On God's sidewalk there was an X scratched
    by hobos.  They knew to come to God's back door and you'd
    get a plate of leftovers and all the sweet tea you could
    drink.  They knew the sugared pints of contentment.  They drank
    sweet tea from God's back steps and went on their wandering
    way again.

For God knows sweet tea fills with love and refreshment from
    any long train.  For sweet tea is safe as an oak forest
    camp.  Sweet tea, clinks in jelly jars.  Sweet tea,
    sweeter as it stands.  For God's sake we brew it
    like religion.  For God's sake we carry it now in styrofoam
    cups in cars.  We drink it in winter.  We drink it always.

And this poem would not lessen sweet tea's place in the creation.
    Sweet tea is not fading from the Southern towns
    like the Confederate flag.  It lives in houses all over town.
    Black folk brew it often as white folk.  Take the flag down off
    the state capitol.  It doesn't mean anything to me.
    But leave me my sweet tea, a recipe for being civil.

This poem stands cold sweet tea up as God's chosen beverage.
    The manifest Southern brew.  When sad I draw figures
    in the condensation of glasses of sweet tea.  I connect
    the grape leaves on the jelly jar, cast out any restaurant

that will not make it from scratch. When lonely I go
to the house of my beloved.

For I love a woman who makes sweet tea late at night to eat with
Chinese food.  For her hands move like God's through the ritual.
For it is as if she had learned it along with speaking in
tongues.  For I love the way her hands unwrap the tea bags
and drop them in the water.  For I love the unmeasured sugar
straight from the bag, the tap water from deep in the earth.
For the processes are as basic as making love.
For our bodies both are brown like suntans inside from years
of tea.  For sweet tea is the Southern land we share, the town,
the past.  When we kiss it is sweet tea that we taste as
our lips brush.  When we are hot it is sweet tea we crave.
When we have children it will be sweet tea.
And they will learn tea along with Bible stories and baseball.

*1995*

# MY DEAD FATHER ON VACATION

I decide I should take my dead father to Myrtle Beach.
That would shut him up. When I bring up the subject,
my dead father says, no, it's just fine right here.
"It's time for you to go home," I say. "Back to the past
from where you came." No, he repeats. I'm just fine.
"You're too comfortable here, I say. "And besides,
my friends are starting to talk."

I convince him to go, and we drive on old back roads
because my dead father doesn't believe in interstates.
We stop at South of the Border, go up in Pedro's tower,
and look out over the flat Carolina farm fields.
"Now this is some country," my dead father says,
staring off into the distance. "This is good tobacco country.
I'm beginning to feel at home." He's happy, so I buy him
a little sombrero, and I even let the attendant
put the bumper sticker on the car.

We get to Myrtle Beach after midnight and head
straight to the Pavilion where he says we can watch
the pretty girls till dawn. "What for?" I ask.
"You'll understand when you've been dead forty years,"
he says, opening a can of Pabst with an old church key.
"They got pop tops now," I say, levering one open.
"They even got laws about old men like you," I joke.
He's not hearing, lost in the parade of flesh and color.

He drinks another beer. I watch my dead father
watch the girls. They can't see him, and it's a good thing,
he's so sloppy drunk.
"Come on," I say. "Time to go home."
"Leave me here," he says. "I'll die happy."
You're already dead, I say, and I drag him to the car.
He's singing some song he learned in the army,
some song with French in it, and I listen, but can't
quite make out the words. The lights spin behind us,
me and my dead father, out on vacation together.

*1997*

# SUSAN LUDVIGSON
## Poetry Fellow, 1983

"The Child's Dream" is one kind of poem I was writing early on, a poem beginning with a childhood incident that segues into adult experience. It's my belief that we don't change very much emotionally, even though we mature and learn to manage (and mask) what we feel in order to present a less vulnerable face to the world. I'm not certain that's a good thing for our souls, but of course it helps us get through the life outside ourselves. I think this idea—that we remain subject to childhood's raw emotions—runs through much of my work even up to the present.

"Man Arrested in Hacking Death" also represents a kind of poem I was writing fairly early. The perverse imagination is caught by stories that demonstrate extremes of human behavior, and I have to admit, I often find humor where others see horror. An earlier series took as its source newspaper articles from the turn of the 19th century. These newspaper pieces illustrate not just the usual murder and mayhem we've come to expect of humankind, but unusually creative ways people can wreak havoc. The actual incidents took place in rural Wisconsin, where I grew up. I assume they grew out of the Scandinavian propensity for the darker sides of things—something I know from the inside. The poem I include here comes from a second series, based on newspaper clippings I stole from a friend's refrigerator door, featuring similarly bizarre stories, this time about men.

"Lasting" is a mid-career poem, written when my increasing awareness of mortality—my own and very possibly the planet's—coincided with my reading of Leonard Shlain's *Art and Physics*. I think most of us yearn for an ending that isn't an ending. I often finish readings with this poem, for its hopefulness, however whimsical.

I write in traditional forms from time to time (most often in terza rima). The central image of "Not Swans," a sonnet, came from a "vision," just as the poem suggests. My father's death in 1977 also led me to write a sonnet, a form that sometimes presents itself when I need a frame for difficult, painful experience.

The recent "Bin Laden in South Carolina" arrived directly from a dream, as more and more of my poems do these days. I am a great believer in the power of the unconscious, and I do all I can to court the muse, who lives in that great repository of metaphor and imagery. The more we pay attention to dreams, the more they repay us with insights and the raw materials for art. I have always used dreams in poem-making, but my reliance on them is greater every year.

Possibly my most characteristic poems are long narrative sequences (too long to include here), but even my newest long poems are shifting toward a more lyrical, less cohesive voice. Is this direction a product of aging? Quite likely.

▲ ▲ ▼ ▲ ▲

Susan Ludvigson's latest collection, *Sweet Confluence, New and Selected Poems*, is her seventh from LSU Press; *Escaping the House of Certainty* is forthcoming, also from LSU Press. Among her awards are fellowships and grants from the Guggenheim, Rockefeller, Witter Bynner and Fulbright foundations and the NEA, as well as the South Carolina Arts Commission and the North Carolina Arts Council. Her poems have been published in some seventy journals, including *Poetry*, *The Atlantic Monthly*, *The Nation*, *Georgia Review*, *Gettysburg Review*, *Virginia Quarterly Review*, *Southern Review*, *Ohio Review*, and *Paris Review*. She has represented the United States at writers' congresses in France, Canada, Belgium, and Yugoslavia. She was poet-in-residence at the University of South Carolina in the spring semester, 2000.

# The Child's Dream

If I could start my life again,
I'd keep the notebook
I promised myself at nine—
a record of all the injustice
done by adults:  that accusing tone
when they speak, the embarrassments
before relatives, like the time
I had to put on my swimsuit in the car
while Mother chatted with an uncle
who peered in, teasing.
And wouldn't they be sorry
later, when they read it,
after I'd been run over by a truck,
their faces darkening
like winter afternoons.
And I, of course (if I survived),
would have a reminder,
in my own hand,
so I'd be the perfect parent,
my children radiant as the northern lights.
It's like poems you hope
will be read by someone who knows
they're for him, and cry
at what he did or didn't do,
wishing to touch your face once more,
to cradle your body.
You can almost hear what he'd tell you
with his voice that sounds
like the sea rolling in
over and over, like a song.

*1978*

## MAN ARRESTED IN HACKING DEATH TELLS POLICE HE MISTOOK MOTHER-IN-LAW FOR RACCOON

Every morning she'd smear something brown
over her eyes, already bagged
and dark underneath, as if that would
get her sympathy.  She never slept,
she said, but wandered like a phantom
through the yard.  I knew it.  Knew
how she knelt beneath our bedroom window too,
and listened to Janet and me.

One night when
*again* Janet said No,
I called her a cow, said she might as well
be dead for all she was good to me.
The old lady had fur in her head
and in her ears,
at breakfast slipped and told us
*she* didn't think the cows would die.

Today when I caught her
in the garage at dawn, that dyed hair
growing out in stripes, eyes
like any animal surprised from sleep
or prowling where it shouldn't be,
I did think, for a minute,
she was the raider of the garden,
and the ax felt good, coming down
on a life like that.

# LASTING

*When the first radio wave music escaped Earth's ionosphere, it literally did become*
*eternal. Music, in this century, has been converted from sound into*
*the clarity of pure light. Radio has superseded the constraints of space.*
                    —Leonard Shlain, Art and Physics

Imagine Vivaldi suddenly falling
on the ears of a woman
somewhere beyond Alpha Centauri,
her planet spun into luminescence
aeons from now.  She might be
much like us, meditating
on the body, her lover murmuring
to the underside of her breast
before its heaviness suspends,
for a moment, the lift and pause
of his breath.  A music she almost knows
drifts through centuries, startling,
augmenting her pleasure.
When earth is particles of dust,
Orson Welles may still strike fear
into the hearts of millions
who wake one morning, unaware
that light has arrived
as an audible prank.  Ezra Pound might rasp
his particular madness from an Italy
still alive in arias that shower
into the open windows
of a world youthful as hope.
When books are no longer even ashes,
and no heart beats in any space
near where we were, suns
may intersect, and some of our voices
blend into choirs, the music of the spheres
adrift among new stars.

*1985*

## Not Swans

I drive toward distant clouds and my mother's dying.
The quickened sky is mercury, it slithers
across the horizon.  Against that liquid silence,
a V of birds crosses—sudden and silver.

They tilt, becoming white light as they turn, glitter
like shooting stars arcing slow motion out of the abyss,
not falling.

       Now they look like chips of flint,
the arrow broken.
        I think, This isn't myth—

they are not signs, not souls.
                 Reaching blue
again, they're ordinary ducks or maybe
Canada geese.  Veering away they shoot
into the west, too far for my eyes, aching

as they do.

       Never mind what I said
before.  Those birds took my breath.  I knew what it meant.

*1999*

# Bin Laden in South Carolina

*It is equal to living in a tragic land*
*To live in a tragic time.*
—Wallace Stevens

We are strolling near the forest when we spot him.
You aim your rifle, he puts his hands up so slowly
he seems to be starting to dance, a dance that begins
in his graceful fingers.

We march him to our house in the meadow,
to the backyard where you tie him
to a chair.

I bring him books.  *Bind his wrists if you must,*
*I plead, but please leave his hands free enough*
*to turn the pages.*  You do not acknowledge
that you've heard me.
I shrug in his direction, reassuring.

I wonder if he reads English.
*He must be bored*, I say, *sitting in the sun*
*for hours*. I think of lemonade,
cold beer.  You growl at me,
"It's you who have been in the sun too long."

My family comes to visit.  They enter the yard
through the gate, a stream of them
carrying casseroles, steaming pies.
As they pass him I whisper who he is.
*Don't stare*, I say.  *You especially*, I hiss
to Aunt Helen, who does.  They all do.
He sees them, lowers his limpid eyes.

I peer out the window, against the rising sun.
*Gone*, I think with a pang.
But I am wrong.  His head lifts
from the damp grass.  He has only been sleeping.

I suggest a more comfortable chair,
offer to go get a cushion.

You stalk behind him, pushing
the barrel into the small of his back.

Your voice is harsh, reminding me
you were a soldier.  You show me the stash
of knives hid in the folds of his robe,
tell me the ropes look loose, I should fix them.
I avert my eyes.

"Do you find him handsome?" my mother asks,
appearing beside me.
*Oh yes*, I think, settling his feet
in the grass, retying the knots.
His hands lie still in his lap.

*What more can I do?*

*Who is responsible? Who shall we call?*
You raise the rifle to your shoulder,
bend to the sight,
tell me to move aside.

*2002*

# TERRI McCORD
## Poetry Fellow, 2002

My poetry has a predilection for transformation. Believing that any action or *any*thing is open to interpretation, I strive for a certain ambiguity in language that I hope works on a concrete level as well as a figurative one and that sparks questions as a result. In "Retribution," I center on a true story of a horrific nature that fascinated me in a visceral stare-at-the-car-wreck way. I wanted to make the horror into a real sacrifice, though, and I try to imply that the resolution of the story lives outside the poem, but hope is there in the "flush of spring."

The occasion for "Dark Side" attracted me because of the potential for word play. On a rural commute, I continually noticed the change of slogans/ ad enticements on a sign for a small tanning business. These slogans reminded me of the ones employed by churches to encourage participation, and so I mingled a tanning bed and religious connotations. This poem has been through numerous revisions because I had a tendency to be too metaphysical with it.

I almost had the opposite challenge with "Sighting," whose genesis began with my actual viewing of a huge white owl in broad daylight. The image was overpowering, but not until I was caring for my sick mother could I create any kind of "story" to go with the vision of the otherworldly owl. At the same time, I wanted to retain a mystical quality to the scene while clarifying it. My experience as a visual artist prompts me to lean heavily on metaphorical language for its emotive and connective potential, so I greatly emphasized the way the bird appeared.

I transform my grandmother into the goddess Diana to illustrate her bravery and, at least in my memory, her immortality, in "Huntress." I think I also chose to use allusion because of the distance created for writing a poem about a difficult, personal subject. That handling of the subject matter, too, I believe, makes the poem more poignant for any reader with a similar experience.

"Winter Stay" is a meditation of sorts on a monochromatic scene with one bead of color that tries to engage the eye as well as the heart with nature. I wanted to make this actual scene more than the black and white photos I shoot, so I studied this stunning woodpecker and decided to transform him into more. I have realized over the years how literally drawn I am to the details of the natural world and nature as well as being fascinated by the transitory nature of things. This poem wants to contemplate that.

▲ ▲ ▼ ▲ ▲

Terri McCord received her B.A. in English from Furman University. She has worked in public relations and has taught creative writing and visual art in a mental health facility, museum programs, and public schools throughout the state (including the Greenville Fine Arts Center and South Carolina Governor's School for the Arts). She is on the South Carolina Arts Commission's Approved Artist Roster for literary and visual arts. She read as part of the poetry panel at the 2002 South Carolina Humanities Book Festival. Ninety-Six Press published a chapbook-sized selection of her poetry in the book *Quintet* in 2003, and her poems have appeared in such literary magazines as *Comstock Review*, *Cimarron Review*, *Yemassee*, and *Cream City Review*. She is currently pursuing an MFA at Queens University in Charlotte.

# Retribution

Maybe he thought
he'd teach his kids
a lesson, like
the crew cuts he gave
against their wills.

Each one watches;
each one sweeps
lost hair from a forehead
as if parting weeds
level with their heads
as they do when playing
hide and seek
in the next door lot.

The half-buried kitten struggles
as the man cranks the motor
on the 20" and slowly wheels
his anger forward
across the cropped lawn.

Told to stand still and close
they huddle, rooted,
shutting their eyelids to
sink into the field,
not to rise until the
first full flush of a spring
and his words, "Go on."

*1995*

## DARK SIDE

The rented signage along the two-lane
appeals to a sense of sin and impatience:
*Get in Touch with Your Dark Side Now!*
next to the cinder block salon, awning
flapping like a blustered beach umbrella.
**T-A-N** stains the painted-white bricks,
the three letters an indelible burn as I pass.
I jerk my short sleeved arm in—veering
the wheel at the fork to Highway Eight.

Still, the invitation stays,
to be vaulted in light
and to eclipse darkness
by shutting the lid,
hiding my fault lines,
until all that is visible is the black
halo of my afterimage,
and what I am now
will have vanished for good.

*1998*

## SIGHTING

It settles outside
her kitchen window, and
startled, she thinks the vision
is herself white-robed, face blanched,
arms outstretched like a sleepwalker
until she grasps the sun is up
and the pane is clear.
The apparition blends with
magnolia blossoms bigger than
hands while its face is wide and telling
like a sundial turned vertical.
The white creature twists its head in
slow increments full circle until
it seems ready to strike—then
the owl spans and shrouds
the window before vanishing.


She hears the rustle from her
mother's bedroom, enters with
the medication and wishes she
*had* seen herself, a lone
and curious angel.

*1999*

# Huntress

The tumor waxes and wanes
in her loosed mind. She misses
the target, hunts for a new word,
calls me by the dog's name,
and I answer. Wheeled
to the hospital center every
morning she wears
a bull's-eye cap pre-measured
for their five-minute practice
six weeks straight only
weekend breaks. Hands spiral
to her side, and stay
until we lift her
onto the backseat, fasten
the buckle, unbutton the sweater
in the summer heat. Then she waves
us away and darts a look
toward home.

After eighty-four
years she has earned the title
of huntress, fierce as Diana
through radiation and final loss
of hair save for a thin pale braid
which crescents on her pink
wrinkled head. My uncle unlocks
the house while I move her from
the car, and she folds into a
broken bow that I take up and
hoist against hip and hold—
until she can rise and look beyond,
trying to protect me again, and
pass on her perfect archer's form.

*2001*

# WINTER STAY

The tree appears to bleed
a single bright drop
as the woodpecker, head lavishly red,
is moved by desire down the limb.
Beneath the branch, the thickly iced
driveway is a clean slate too
hard to mark as I remain inside
the study. The bird continues
to bore in a straight descending line,
etching the naked bark—
the trunk a great god's pointing
finger pricked now and poised
for some sort of blood bond—
until he tires of the wait and lifts away,
leaving the tree to stand frozen
and gray, a monochrome print untouched.

*2004*

# John Ower
## Poetry Fellow, 1977

The poems I wrote before 1998 have without doubt a certain artistic merit. However, I have come to regard them as being "overwrought" in both senses of the word, as morbid and primarily of psychiatric interest. I have therefore selected for this anthology only representative examples of my recent work as a haiku poet. Most of the pieces I have chosen are from my recent volume *Winter Touch* (Hub Press: UK, 2001). I have also included two unpublished haiku inspired by the landscape of the South. Most of my little poems should speak for themselves; however, I will note that "in burnished stone" refers to the Vietnam War Memorial in Washington, D.C. It will also be helpful to the reader to know that the "emerald jewel scarabs" arose from my communing with the site of one of the bloodiest battles of the Civil War (34,000 casualties). "Scarabs" turns upon a subconsciously generated nexus of comparisons and contrasts between the heavily but powerfully flying beetles and the bone-shattering leaden Minié rifle ball. One of the oppositions is that between the gorgeous insects, swarming to mate, and the Minié slug as an ugly, death-dealing travesty of the human *glans penis*.

▲▲▼▲▲

John Ower was born in New Zealand but has spent most of his time in the Canadian West and in the American South. He is a retired university professor of English Literature, who has taught in Canada, New Zealand, and the United States. He currently lives with his wife, Marian, in Hattiesburg, Mississippi. His poems have appeared in over one hundred magazines and anthologies in a number of countries. A volume of his "mainstream" verse, *Legendary Acts*, was published by the University of Georgia Press in 1977. A gathering of his haiku, *Winter Touch*, appeared in 2001 from the Hub Press as part of its haiku series. Ower has also published numerous articles and notes on literary topics. He lives surrounded by antiques and artworks from Japan and other countries. He has a wide variety of aesthetic and intellectual interests, including the study of natural history.

spring day—an
undertaker's
burnishing his hearse's
black

winter touch—
between us snapping
unexpected spark

our spindly shadows
on the snow—
shortest winter day

since the auto wreck—
profounder purple, morning
glories
with more vivid blue

with summer morning
luminous—
a firefly's wings

one sunset closer
to my death—this crimson
in the clouds

coyote prints—
dark across my lawn's
morning dew

February noon—
the Spanish moss
half-blended with its light

TV evangelist
vanishes—
the thunder

dead fly—
resting on
its wings

backfire—
ghetto children
scatter

just before
the stars—
fireflies
rising

after my optometrist
the cherry blossoms
blind


riverbank—
with half its roots
an oak is holding on


sunny winter morning
its shadows white
with rime


in burnished stone
behind the names—
the living vet's reflection


emerald jewel scarabs
so  many flying heavily
in Chickamauga's meadows

# RON RASH
### Poetry Fellow, 1991

B rendan Galvin claims that "in poetry clarity is the deepest mystery of all." From the beginning, I have tried to write poems that support Galvin's premise. I want my poems to be like a mountain trout stream—clear but with depths not at first apparent. Such an attempt is "July, 1949," an early poem published in my first collection, *Eureka Mill*, and is typical of most of my later work as well in its being set in a specific place, the Carolina mountains. "One place understood helps us understand all other places better," Eudora Welty has said, and she is right, for one of the most interesting aspects of literature is how the most intensely regional writing is often the most universal, as can be seen in our language's two living Nobel-Prize poets, Derek Walcott and Seamus Heaney. The best regional writers are like farmers drilling for water—if they bore deep and true enough into a particular place, beyond the surface of local color, they tap into universal correspondences. I cannot imagine a time when I will not write about the region where my family has lived since the mid-1700s.

There have been changes in my poetry, however, and the biggest one began in the early 1990s when I began a study of traditional Welsh poetics. I was particularly drawn to Welsh poetry's emphasis on the interplay of sound within a line, what the Welsh called *cynhunned*. One of the dangers in being a narrative poet is that the poems can become little more than chopped-up prose. I wanted to write narrative poems with a lyric intensity, and I came to believe I could best achieve this intensity by, to use Hopkins' word, "chiming" consonants and vowels both across and within my lines. I began using a shorter line (seven syllables, another aspect learned from traditional Welsh poetry) as another way to intensify my work. In my second book, *Among the Believers*, most of the poems incorporate aspects of Welsh poetry, as in the poems "The Corpse Bird" and "The Exchange." Perhaps some of my receptivity to Welsh poetics is genetic, for the Rash family migrated to the southern Appalachians from Wales. For whatever reason, I have continued to write poems in this vein, as is evident in "Black-eyed Susans," a poem from my third book, *Raising the Dead*.

▲ ▲ ▼ ▲ ▲

Ron Rash is the author of three books of poetry: *Eureka Mill*, *Among the Believers* and *Raising the Dead*. In 1994 he won an NEA Poetry Fellowship. He is the John Parris Chair in Appalachian Studies at Western Carolina University and lives in Clemson, South Carolina. His first novel, *One Foot in Eden*, won numerous honors, including *Foreword Magazine's* Best Literary Novel for 2002. His most recent novel, *Saints at the River*, was released by Henry Holt and Company in summer 2004. Both novels were read on NPR's Radio Reader program.

# July, 1949

This is what I cannot remember—
a young woman stooped in a field,
the hoe callousing her hands,
the rows stretching out like hours.
And this woman, my mother, rising
to dust rising half a mile
up the road, the car
she has waited days for
realized in the trembling heat.

It will rust until spring, the hoe
dropped at the field's edge.
She is running toward the car,
the sandlapper relatives who spill out
coughing mountain air with lint-filled lungs,
running toward the half-filled grip
she will learn to call suitcase.

She is dreaming another life,
young enough to believe
it can only be better—
indoor plumbing, eight hour shifts, a man
who waits unknowing for her, a man
who cannot hear through the weaving room's
roar the world's soft click,
fate's tumblers falling into place,
soft as the sound of my mother's
bare feet as she runs,
runs toward him, toward me.

*1990*

# THE EXCHANGE

Between Wytheville, Virginia
and the North Carolina line,
he meets a wagon headed
where he's been, seated beside
her parents a dark-eyed girl
who grips the reins in her fist,
no more than sixteen, he'd guess
as they come closer and she
doesn't look away or blush
but allows his eyes to hold
hers that moment their lives pass.
He rides into Boone at dusk,
stops at an inn where he buys
his supper, a sleepless night
thinking of fallow fields still
miles away, the girl he might
not find the like of again.
When dawn breaks he mounts his roan,
then backtracks, searches three days
hamlets and farms, any smoke
rising above the tree line
before he heads south, toward home,
the French Broad's valley where spring
unclinches the dogwood buds
as he plants the bottomland,
come night by candlelight builds
a butter churn and cradle,
cherry headboard for the bed,
forges a double-eagle
into a wedding ring and then
back to Virginia and spends
five weeks riding and asking
from Elk Creek to Damascas
before he finds the wagon
tethered to the hitching post
of a crossroads store, inside
the girl who smiles as if she'd
known all along his gray eyes
would search until they found her.
She asks one question, his name,
as her eyes study the gold

smoldering there between them,
the offered palm she lightens,
slips the ring on herself so
he knows right then the woman
she will be, bold enough match
for a man rash as his name.

*1998*

# THE CORPSE BIRD

Bed-sick she heard the bird's call
fall soft as a pall that night
quilts tightened around her throat,
her gray eyes narrowed, their light
gone as she saw what she'd heard
waiting for her in the tree
cut down at daybreak by kin
to make the coffin, bury
that perch around her so death
might find one less place of rest.

*1998*

## BLACK-EYED SUSANS

The hay was belt-buckle high
when rain let up, three-days' sun
baked stalks dry, and by midday
all but the far pasture mowed,
raked into wind rows, above
June sky still blue so I drove
my tractor up on the ridge
to the far pasture where strands
of sagging barbed wire marked where
my land stopped, church land began,
knowing I'd find some grave-gift,
flowers, flag, styrofoam cross
blown on my land, and so first
walked the boundary, made sure what
belonged on the other side
got returned, soon enough saw,
black-eyed susans, the same kind
growing in my yard, tied to
the bow a tight-folded note.
*Always* was all that it said,
which said enough for I knew
what grave that note belonged to,
and knew as well who wrote it,
she and him married three months
when he died, now always young,
always their love in first bloom,
too new to life to know life
was no honeymoon.  Instead,
she learned that lesson with me
over three decades, what fires
our flesh set early on cooled
by time and just surviving,
and learned why old folks called it
getting hitched, because like mules
so much of life was one long row
you never saw the end of,
and always he was close by,
under a stone you could see
from the porch, wedding picture
she kept hid in her drawer,
his black-and-white flash-bulb grin

grinning at me like he knew
he'd made me more of a ghost
to her than he'd ever be.
There at that moment—that word
in my hand, his grave so close,
if I'd had a shovel near
I'd have dug him up right then,
hung his bones up on the fence
like a varmint, made her see
what the real was, for memory
is always the easiest
thing to love, to keep alive
in the heart. After awhile
I lay the note and bouquet
where they belonged, never spoke
a word about it to her
then or ever, even when
she was dying, calling his
name with her last words. Sometimes
on a Sunday afternoon
I'll cross the pasture, make sure
her stone's not starting to lean,
if it's early summer bring
black-eyed susans for her grave,
leave a few on his as well,
for soon enough we'll all be
sleeping together, beyond
all things that ever mattered.

*2001*

# S. PAUL RICE
## Poetry Fellow, 1996

In 1845 English polymath William Whewell wrote:

> *We probably never will be able to demonstrate what was that*
> *primitive state of things from which the progressive course of the*
> *world took its first departure. In all cases the path is lost in obscurity*
> *as it is traced backwards towards its starting point. It becomes not*
> *only invisible, but unimaginable; it is not only an interruption,*
> *but an abyss, which interposes itself between us and any intelligible*
> *beginning of things.*

As a member of the last minority group that can still be publicly ridiculed, I, as a Southern white man, have assiduously tried to avoid all the straits and narrows that have been created to "civilize" me and make me respectable: the one-size-fits-all poetic of the Master of Fine Arts degree; the marginalizing of our poet laureate, James Dickey, one of the finest bards to ever ring the "iron of English"; the painfully earnest chronicle of the confessional poets and their hangers-on. Southern men have been stripped of our political heritage; we have been chided by the politically correct into treading upon the porcelain shells of language lest we offend some delicate little sensibility somewhere. The story of Post-modern poetry is a narrative of disconnection and trivialization, and I disavowed it long ago.

I grew up on a working farm in central Georgia, the son of a cotton mill family on my father's side and a sawmill family on my mother's. We grew beans and canned them. We killed rabbits and ate them. About a quarter mile down the road from my house, near the Big Spring, lay a field that had been home to ten thousand years of Indian villages. I found my first flint spearhead in that red clay when I was five. It penetrated my imagination and has been embedded there ever since. It was made by a man whose name I do not know, a maker who reached out to me over six thousand years to a land we now call Harris County. This artist had a name; he joked, sang songs, told stories, knapped flint, and he died.

The woods and fields are full of medicinal plants, but our slender and painful Post-modern lyrics don't know what to call them or what they can cure. The hepatica, the button snakeroot, the dock weed have lost their faces and their names.

My great-great-grandfather, Joseph Addison Winchester, a private in the Confederate Army, was wounded at Chickamauga and finished his tour lying on a cot in a Columbus hospital. He was mustered out in 1864, and in 1904 his elements were returned to the soil of Georgia. I have asked to be buried by his side.

I place my poetry in the middle of all this. I want to wake up in the dark and light the stove. I want to eat rattlesnake muscle for supper. I want to grab the fallen power line, even if it kills me.

My hope for my poetical self is that I in some small way can help build a bridge over the abyss, to help reconnect the art of poetry to its elemental beginnings. I desperately want to prove Whewell wrong. I pray for imagination.

Paul Rice has the MFA in creative writing from the University of Arkansas, with a concentration in poetry, and the Ph.D. in English from The Catholic University of America, with a specialization in 20th-century British and American poetry and poetic theory. He has won numerous awards for his poetry including the Southern Literary Festival Poetry Prize, the Atlanta Writing Center Chapbook Award, the *Arts Journal* poetry prize, a *Kudzu* poetry contest award, and the Amon Liner Award of *The Greensboro Review*. Also he was a winner in the South Carolina Fiction Project competition. He has work (poems, reviews, and scholarly and feature articles) in *Poetry*, *Kansas Quarterly*, *The Georgia Review*, *Southern Humanities Review*, *The Chronicle of Higher Education*, *The Mother Earth News*, *The Chattahoochee Review*, and dozens of others.

Paul Rice died suddenly on October 17, 2004 in Conway, South Carolina.

## Erato Howling: The Lyric Muse Takes Back Her Land

I've got a slim, slim waist and big old arms.
I've got piss in my pistols,
lizards in my liquor.
and I've come to take back my home.

I.

look upon my metonymy monster truck,
you blued-haired poetry suckers, you tweed-eating
metrical uncles and despair.
I have cruise metaphors
aimed at your poetry societies.
I have archetypal spears to stick in your patè.

I will shit in your poetical parlors,
JetSki in your watery diction
and drive my lead-treaded images over acres
of your verbal Wedgwood.

I will build huge Majolica prisons
and hold you there forever in chains of dull rhyme.
Look at the poetic diction on my sweatshirt
it says "strangle the whole bunch of platitude-puking,
aphorism-eating, lyric lickers ere they pen again"

II.

Look upon my atomic trope-soaked tampons
you dysmenorrheic suburban MFA's,
you pasta cranking health-club, thigh-blasting
digressive debutante dilettantes,
who make the two-backed beast
with Nautilus machine,
you,
Yale Younger Puppets,
cult of St. Helen of Vendler,
plathsextonlowell wannabes
whose slightest neural twitter

over prunes and dry toast
become ten self-obsessive skinny lyrics
by noon the same day,
squeezed out like little candy coated rabbit turds

III.

And This is for you leather-patched tenured poets,
who stand tall above workshops
who visit incessantly poetically
you who suck wind through the O's in "Iowa Program".

I will put rat-heart rhythm in your Jim Beam
and make you drink it
till your tongue is coated with fur,
and till you, desperate, come out of your windowless offices
and out to the scop-altar where the storm is laid.

Look upon the light from my millennial word-horde
you buttermilk enemaed language poets
you chocolate-smeared cutting edge, avant
garde,
yadda noise, codsack cut and wind-penis

look upon my rainbow skin you ideological MLA myth midgets.
I will set your roads with jargon mines.
the hegemonic mine will jump up head-level
and blow your jawbone clear across the river.
the postcolonial mine will jump up your ass
and blow small golden conquistadors out through your belly.
I will set my multicultural word-cavalry
on your mind's Harvard Honkies
and butcher them in their anti-Platonic potlatches.
I will set my word-Comanches on your mind's settler children.
Irony-Indians will dance far into the night
with strings of blond scalps bloody,
and  necklaces of blue eyeballs.

stick your finger in the poem-socket
and touch your deepest dark wet organ.
you can make

vegetarians wear the sign of the T-bone.
carnivores will sleep at night in soy-bean mud.
your shirt will drip dragon spit,
Grendel-semen, and the wonderous ichor of Kraken

And when I take back my beach
I will open a sky-writer wind-chariot postpaper.
every minute I will publish raptor talon runes
in clouds against a sky of blue fire,
in gem-colored flame against a ocean of onyx,
I will write this on the asses of critics in editor blood:

       beauty is teeth, teeth beauty.
       that's why Rintrah roars,
       And why the moving hand shakes fire.

*1990*

## HAVING MY FATHER'S NAME WRITTEN ON MY FOREHEAD

seven coffins for the seven dead
seventy roads to the godhead

which one runs down this home road
where the clay is blood red?
what exegete can explicate the code?
let Samuel the Prophet try.

what does "Samuel" mean?

ASKED OF GOD.

it came to me in a dream
written in tobacco spit
on a field of briars.

Samuel is my name,
was my father's name.

what is the Father's name?
it is tetragrammaton

God, what a load I have taken on.

*2004*

# LOOKING HOMEWARD

*for Thomas Wolfe and beginning with a line from Richard Hugo*


you <u>can</u> go home again
but you'll arrive one day late for salvage,

and you'll find that the farm
stretching from behind your memory
up and over the wide heroic sky
is become a few scrub acres
of run red clay and stunted oak.

your favorite childhood elm still stands,
but it has no leaves on its bones;
gnawing things have picked your grandfather's barn
to a skeleton of rotten timbers
beneath a rattling skin of rusty metal.

you can go home again
but you'll arrive one day late
for those emerald watermelons
with meat of real rubies,
seeds of real onyx,
for the blackberry pies with crusts of burnished gold,
filled with sugared garnets.

you'll find that buzzards circle high above,
making a black cosmology,
a constellation negative against the late afternoon.
they settle among distant pines
as the sun plays its last trick.
you might even find they weren't birds at all
but a Libra, a Virgo of floaters,
junk the turning years have left in your ocular jelly.

you can go home again,
but there you'll remember
sending your childhood kite a message,
how the wind pushed the words up the string.
you told the kite there was no end to April,
that it was a hawk with a belly full of sun dogs
and no need to hunt, forever.

if you could tell the kite today
what would you say?

that your grandmother who called you in from spring
has become the name on your grandmother's stone,
that her turnip greens and green-apple cobbler

have become the green of her grass,
that the cotton mill girls, your aunts,
now lie in rows like spinning-frames,
while the mill looks on with empty eyes
and dust on its breath?

it won't matter what you tell the kite.
it has tangled its wings in power lines
and rain has washed its feathers into ditches.

       time is a river is a clichè.
       if time is a stream
       it's a dry creek
       with the blue cats
       bloated belly up in the mud
       and stinking.
       time is not a river.
       time is a son of a bitch.
       it is all those creatures grinning in the dirt,
       waiting to steal the flesh from your hands
       even while you stroke the hair of someone you love.

       time is not a river.
       time is a short stick
       that takes long years to beat you to death.

yeah, you can go home again
but why would you try?
better to ride the interstates at night
with your headlights on dim
and the radio up so loud
you just can't hear your mind remember.

*2000*

# THE SWIMMER AND THE SEA

*for Laura*

I.

the autumn sea has grey skin;
it is wrinkled with the ages;
it has grey hair, speaks quietly,
and knows a great deal about time.
already, a billion years ago the sea was old.

II.

the young woman confronts the sea.
she flings herself,
an argument against old breakers.
she has a swimmer's shoulders.
her skin is as brown
as the sea is grey.
her red swimsuit contradicts
the ocean's smoky green.
wave after wave she dives headlong,
strong and bronze.

III.

the old woman has grey skin, grey hair.
she speaks quietly;
her whispers have the sea's sibilance.
her gown is grey,
and the walls of her room
rise from grey floors.
she does not notice the saline drip.
she does not remember the red swimsuit.
the ocean does not echo in her broken shell.

IV.

the summer sea has strong shoulders.
there is new sun on the Atlantic
and the water has bronze skin, red/gold hair.
the sea has strong arms

and flings its salt at the land.
it speaks to the sand in a voice like drums.

in a billion years
the sea will still be young.

*1970*

# Three Hieroglyphs Containing the Symbol for Crow

I.       Rain Crow

good morning.
the rain that flies at us
like eighth-notes wakes us up.
there is some rain singing to the roof.
listen.
rain is the song summer uses
to lull our houses into carelessness.
rain molds the clapboard,
mildews the plaster,
and when rain goes into the dirt
it takes our home in increments.
our lives are in the dark aquifer
in parts.

>        when the rain has gone
>        then the rain crow sings.
>        the song says that what seems the same
>        is really so much less a thing.
>
>        the rain crow is sound's rainbow.
>        it tells the biggest lie.
>        it would have us think of hope
>        when what it really means is
>
>        goodbye.


II.      Crow's Feet  (A Song)

>        hello.
>        crow's feet
>        are what the years have used
>        to clock her face.
>        time has cornered her with its eyes.

some year or the other
she awoke with skin
that went less well with lace
that it once did
when in sandals and liquid linen skirts

she flowed with an amazing grace.

hello. come in.
this morning's neighbors at the door
with covered dishes
make a festive matins
that counterpoints
the formal oratory of her box
and its eloquent satins.
what seems sleep has taken the crow's feet
completely from her eyes.
she looks so good.
her neighbors,
children, husband gather for their
goodbyes.
and then the gathering flies.


III.    Crowbar

happy new year.
decay is the only calendar we need.
a long time has passed
when it's time to tear down the house,
even if those decades were like no time at all.

the crowbar prizes the window sills
where lace sleeves have leaned.
the crowbar prizes door-frames
stained with greeting and parting.
the crowbar prizes the lintel
where the mistletoe hung.
and breaks the heart-pine floor

that remembers every word
of The Story of Children's Feet.

the crowbar and the backhoe
finish what the weather has begun.
the crowbar is time's iron telegram,
sings
goodbye.
and then the circling carrion birds
scrawl their elegies across the sky.

*1980*

# WARREN SLESINGER
### Poetry Fellow, 2002

Although we are not responsible for our dreams, we need to accept them for what they are: a form of thought, if not a form of self-analysis. I know that I wanted to merge with the moonlight when I dreamed about

"Our Bedroom in the Fields," but I am not sure what to make of the mirror in the middle of the path or the figure that I found there. I suppose that it replicates the sense of strangeness whenever we encounter "the other" in our dreams or elsewhere.

I spent a lot of time in hotels and motels when I was an editor, and I often found myself listening to the people in these places whether I wanted to hear them or not. One weekend, deep in paperwork, I overheard a conversation in another room, and it prompted me to write "The Virtue of Loneliness." There is a bit of introspection in the poem together with an awareness of the woman upstairs, the people next door and the noises in the street. Of course, it is a sestina, in which the same words are rhymed in a set pattern, which is "right" for the feeling of confinement that always draws me outdoors.

At this point, I wish that I could say that writing comes easy, but it never does. I began and abandoned "The Ring of Dancers" so often that I lost count. It was not a sense of "urgency" that made me return to it, but a recurrent dream. It seemed to me that if I pursued it, if I inquired into it, I might learn something about myself and the world. I know that motivation is no measure of success, but I believe that I matured in the process. At least I am able to see myself more objectively and the poem more subjectively as a means of discovery.

Although I was raised in the Midwest, I came of age on the East Coast, and I would not like to live more than a day's drive from the ocean. What I wanted to replicate in "Never Simple or Still" was how the waves and the interplay of wind, clouds and light are a constant distraction. At the same time, there is something so forceful about the sea that its restless energy regenerates the whole thought process. The man in the poem holds himself accountable for something that he would rather forget, but if conscience is a mind that watches itself, there is no escape from it.

I went on field trips with the writers and photographers at the South Carolina wildlife magazine because I was responsible for manuscripts that dealt with the state's natural resources when I was an editor at the university press. Since then, I have taken a couple of master naturalist courses and learned more about the complex system that supports and sustains us. I wrote "Wheat" on a return trip from the Midwest where the landscape was changed as much as ours was when indigo and rice were grown on such a grand scale in the Lowcountry. Although I am not a "nature" writer, I care about the environment almost as much as I do about personal relationships.

▲ ▲ ▼ ▲ ▲

Warren Slesinger graduated from the Iowa Writers Workshop with an MFA, then taught English part-time while working full-time in the publishing business as an editor, marketing manager or sales manager at the following university presses: Chicago, Oregon, Pennsylvania and South Carolina. He has received an Ingram Merrill grant and his poetry has been published in *The American Poetry Review*, *The Antioch Review*, *The Beloit Poetry Journal*, *The Georgia Review*, *The Iowa Review*, *The Nation*, *New Letters*, *The North American Review*, *Northwest Review*, *Poetry Daily*, *The Sewanee Review*, and *The South Carolina Review*. He has been in residence at the Yaddo and MacDowell colonies for writers, and the Sitka Center for the Study of the Arts and Environment.

# Our Bedroom in the Fields

We went from the woods to the walls
when the moon stood steep in the ceiling
of our bedroom in the fields.

                              We lived in a land
of beds and dressers with a mirror in the middle
of the path, a stand of trees where the moonlight
falls from the woods to the walls in soft shafts.

We loved the notched blooms above the baseboard
of our bedroom in the fields: the spines, the spikes
and the star-like spars that cracked in back
of the woodwork when we moved toward the mirror
in the middle of the path.

                              We let a spider
in the creekbed when we pried apart the weeds.

We wanted to touch the nuts and berries
on the bedframe, if the mirror made them
more remarkable in wood and glass
than the figure in the middle of the path,
the moonlight—even the dust is the depth
of its own reflection;

                              we wanted to touch
a panoply of leaves, if the mirror made them
more remarkable in wood and glass
than the meek pronouncements when we meet


the eyes that water with their weakness
and their wrong—even the dust is the depth
of its own reflection:

                              the landscape locked in solid rock
and stock-still trees while the heavens hardened above us,
and the path narrowed to a point where we made love.

# THE VIRTUE OF LONELINESS

Through the afternoon in the old, brown roses that papered
the walls of the room, he slept with one eye open. The window
was a point of view without a point of view behind it: clear glass,
a strong light, and clean curtains. Without a woman,
he slept in his own sweat. He heard the handle
of a drawer, other voices in other rooms, the noises in the street.

But he never went into the street. His hand
held a pencil out of habit or moved a paperweight
when he wrote about a dream in the head of a beautiful woman;
a golden meadow lost in its own harmony; a voice from the window
of a room that was not his own. The street sign
was difficult to read at such a distance. Without his glasses,

he never went beyond the range of his own voice. The glass
would vibrate, but it would never break. He knew it was a woman
when he heard the hangers in the closet overhead, tissue paper
in a box, the silken rush of underthings when she walked to the window,
her heels on the hardwood floor. Before she reached the street,
if he could only hold her underneath him in the sheets, her hands

and arms around him while he was humpbacked on his hands
and knees. The people were passing through the street.
He heard the grince of the grain on the pavement, a newspaper
that the neighbors packed into a barrel of dishes and glassware;
the huff of the lift as high as the window,
and the lumbering grunt of the load; the voice of the woman

who owned the apartment and the voice of the man
with a splinter from the barrel in his hand
that she offered to examine. The eyes are the windows
of the soul in a book of poetry, if the soul is a woman
with a man's face and a man's voice, but it broke in his throat like glass.
The whole neighborhood would know about the room with a window

instead of a door, the sign with the illegible letters, the street
that gave the geography no meaning, the life behind the glass.
He had written a letter to the newspaper about the man

and the woman who took him by the hand. The whole street
was gossiping about it. The answer came with his name in the window
of an envelope like an open secret:

The virtue of loneliness is nothing to keep.

# THE RING OF DANCERS

It was a land in league with its own remoteness;
a land half-sea; the sea, half-ledge
on a course that he had chosen when he crossed over a thousand
mapped square miles of openness:
water and wind that carried the clouds toward an island
so far north of the norm that it was known
by its coordinates instead of a name for what he wanted:
a world in the reach of his rigging.

Instead of spillways, a place with hills where the pines stood still.
On the porch that overlooked the harbor,
he could light his pipe and rock as slowly as the boat that rode
below him on the ripples of its own reflection.

He watched a wave lift and pound itself to spray.
Where in the world with its gulls and its garbage was the shore?
It was not on the horizon that dipped and drew the eye
that watched the whitecaps and the sky into a network of wrinkles
while the map was flapping in his hand, and he tried to locate
this windspit of sand, this island in the North Atlantic
that traded with the traffic of the screeching birds.

He let go of the wheel, and the sea steered him
over the lifting swell toward the clanging dome of the bell buoy
that rolled above and below him with one cold stroke
of the tide, and the coastline came through the mist
crumbling from its cliffs.

At the landing, his sea-legs sagged.
The wake of everywhere that he had been caught up with him
in plunging undulations that washed and washed among the pilings
as if the sea could not come clean of something.

It was a large world in a small place.
A church pointed a wooden steeple at the sky above a cluster
of clapboard houses. The women knotted their kerchiefs,
the men pulled at their caps. It was bright enough to see a bead
of pinesap in a board, and the sand in the street
was as clean and coarse as salt, but he smelled the odor of fish

from the barrels in a wagon to the nets on the dock,
to the flies in the toilet where the urine spattered in the stall.

Outside, he saw a fisherman pluck his pipe
from his mouth, and spit in the wind for luck.


In a store, he bought a postcard and a sweater
at a bargain table from a blue-eyed blond with braids
and a smile as wide as the rippling tide.
He wanted to nibble at her neck with white bites
when she explained the rate of exchange,
but he could tell that he would lose his money
because the bell in back of the door
clattered and clanged like a piece of loose change.

He inquired about a sign that he had seen of people
dancing in a ring, and she replied that it signified their life
together on the island. It was the folkdance of the fishermen.
They performed it once a week just to keep the tourists
from leaving. Indeed, he had seen it stamped in purple
on his passport and the price tags in the store.
It appeared on dinner plates with epigrams and the borders
of bedspreads, tablecloths and napkins. It was in the knit
of winter mittens and matching caps. The figures of the dancers
were as tightly woven as the social order.

Outside, the sun was setting in the pines. He shivered
in his sweater that unraveled as he walked away.

On a stony outcrop where the goats grazed,
he watched a wave that summed itself up to nothing
as it crested and collapsed. Where in the world
with its knives and its nets was the haul?

At a tavern on a distant strand, the dark of the carpet
came to his knees. The women whispered;
the men puffed on their pipes and watched him
while he ate the local dish. He gave a great red gasp
when he drank the wine that stripped the lining from his throat,
and heard them joke about the time of the tide
and the feeding depth of fish.

In the window was a world that tipped and spilled.
The moon appeared too near and bright as a bulb
lit by a chain in a room too small to hold all the people
who nudged him toward the middle of the ring
where the blonde slipped her hand into his and kissed him
with her lips wet and her earrings jingling.

He stiffened at the rigid fiddling; he trembled on the trill
of the tinny whistle until the drumbeat struck him dumb.
He staggered, the line sagged; the moon rolled over his shoulder,
and the hands of the dancers caught him
when he came to the surface of the roundabout world.

# NEVER SIMPLE OR STILL

Save for the shorebirds, the beach is empty,
the barren sandbars cold, and the sea in the offing,
the sea that shimmers in the light from a high overcast,
tumbles in and out, together and against itself.

But for the blaze of memory, the man out walking
would not be on the beach at all. He has long since
lost interest in looking for something to pick up:
stone, bottle or shells.

Nor is the distance or direction of his walk
of interest or the day itself, if it reminds him
of a place like this still plainly visible
in his consciousness when he squints

at the recollection of lotion on the shoulders
of a girl with small breasts in a skin-tight suit
with slipped straps; her skin pink, his fingers slick
with lotion; its sweet-tipped scent in the salt air

and sunshine on a hidden beach in the heat
of a summer that remains within the reach
and retreat of his memory, but the dunes are drab
in the winter, the grasses bent by the wind thus far,

and apart from the interplay of wind, clouds,
and light, the sea is never simple or still,
but the way, his way, is always the same
from one end of the beach to the other

in a daze and she not sharply defined;
her hair a brownish blur, her face plain,
her eyes straining to find if he meant
to quit and leave her entirely, and yet,

he remembers that bare little body
chilly with sweat and the dampness of sex
when the swirling water forms a trough
that drains the colors from the shells,

while the tide ebbs, and the oyster beds
seem to shudder in the surge, and slide forward
in the lull; the sea to withhold, and hurl itself
at the shore again, and his remorse has no resolution.

# WHEAT

Outside of town, you pull off the road
at a wayside with the clearest view of the county:
square-topped fields of high-yield wheat
that once were rock-ribbed hills; sunlit blocks

of silence without a house or barn on land,
it seems, too large to farm—save for the equipment
that crosses it in tandem: the air glimmering
with ground-up dust when an International Harvester

turns with a surge of its engine and propels the blades
in the opposite direction. The hills absorb the sunlight
as the machinery moves downwind, and the silence
of the former woods and forgotten streams settles in again.

The utility poles and power lines that parallel the road
seem to waver for an instant, and begin to bunch together
in a tangle of their own multitude like a knot in the middle
of nothing but the road and the toppled grain;

the terminus of the next ten minutes of driving,
and still the distance to another range of redirected streams
and retreating hills; mile after mile of farm property,
and a prosperity that lies beyond the purchase of your eyes.

—for Joe Sanders

# KATHLEEN WHITTEN
## Poetry Fellow, 1995

"Your life is a poem," said a collage artist at the Lee Park Arts Festival in Charlottesville, Virginia. Her St. George and the Dragon sat ten feet from a three-times-life-size verdigris bronze statue of Robert E. Lee on Traveler. So, yes, we did stand at the center of a poem in that moment, the moment where every poem erupts, especially in the moments when there are too many absurdities and contradictions for one mind to hold, to order.

What else can I say about "my life as a poet," as I was asked to for this book? I live life as a psychologist, mother, teacher, writer, wife—and I write poems. The strands of those roles grow in tendrils around the poems. An important part of my life as a poet is engagement in the world—the world's needs for social justice, for international relief, for mothering, for teaching, for giving voice to those who have been silenced. That engagement launches me into situations with no apparent connection—on Dong Khoi Street in Saigon, now Ho Chi Minh City; at the Red Cross blood donation center; in the swept yard of a woman who lost her child. Themes? That's a comp-lit term for obsessions. Here are mine: sudden transformations; Vietnam, both the American War and the country of my daughter's birth; and the American South of small towns, as I remember them from the 1950s and 1960s.

Psychology has its own explanations for everything. Psychologists have standardized diagnoses, statistical techniques for analysis, advanced quantitative methods, reliable and valid measures. But at the end of the day, when I close the books and files and turn off the computers, I return home to the glorious riot of the inexplicable, my true spiritual home; to the land of poetry, a crystal city where everything is clear, even if it cannot be fully explained. Where language is its own reward—and where the lyric poem gives the best possible explanation for the contradictory and absurd condition of the world. A science of linear quantitative methods cannot hold them, but poems can. That's why I write poems. The personal lyric is like an unfired clay bowl that stretches and shapes itself to fit the material inside it. Words arrange themselves into unique voices. The voices whisper hints of meaning beyond language. Poetry bridges psychological science and nonverbal spiritual life. Poetry reflects that life like mirrors held out to see around blind corners.

Be ready. Every moment is a possible poem.

▲ ▲ ▼ ▲ ▲

Kathleen Whitten's poetry has appeared in *Negative Capability*, *The Graham House Review*, the *Journal of the American Medical Association*, and others. She was on the South Carolina Readers' Circuit and taught poetry and creative nonfiction for the state's Arts-in-Education program. She was a columnist for *The State* newspaper and has written video scripts produced by SCETV. She received her Ph.D. in psychology from the University of Virginia, where she now works in the Department of Psychiatric Medicine. She lives with her husband and daughter in Charlottesville, Virginia.

# DONG KHOI STREET

The toothless mother is not too thin
to make milk for her baby, does not squat
on worn flip-flops in the tailor's door.

The baby does not creep on bare knees
and feet across broken concrete
when she is old enough to walk.

I did not spend more on my baby's
adoption than this woman will ever see.

The young man does not balance an entire window
on his back as he pedals. Something more
than a thin layer of rubber and air
holds him on his bicycle.

The rubber did not come from sap
the fever of trees, the product
vulcanized with blood.
*Ce sont mes coolis. C'est tout.*
Before Tet meant Offensive.

The Cathedral of Notre Dame, four blocks away,
does not keep the God imported from France
captured in a cracker under a neon crucifix.

The old man does not lean against the tailor's door jamb,
does not pull up his frayed hem to show
his oozing sore, does not hold out his brown hand
to the Americans inside.

I am not that American, even though the tailor
measures me for a fuchsia silk *ao dai*.
Besides, the agency said not to give money to beggars.

The boy who should be in school
does not run in with a necklace of postcards,
"Madame, madame, you buy, you buy,
only 10,000 dong."

I am not Madame.
God does not sleep under neon.

Kwan Yin, goddess of mercy,
hangs from taxi mirrors,
stands banyan-tall before pagodas.
Monks invite gongs to bring us back to our selves.
When it's too hot to breathe,
the narrow way of breath must be enough.

*2002*

# Charge of the Nightingale

*Today the poet must learn to lead a charge.*
—Nguyen That Tan, a.k.a. Ho Chi Minh

I. Savannah, 1969

Wet kisses in Mama's hall until
the Huey pilot's erection stood to
like a salute in his olive flight suit.
He shipped out soon after to Vietnam.

It looked like south Georgia
from the air, they said—
bright green marshes of Spartina grass
interrupted by dark dense splotches of live oaks,
palmetto trees like coconut palms.
Ideal for pilot training. And the heat.
"Tropical" tells you nothing. Just-showered air, never dry,
swamps of cypress, water moccasins, webs of Spanish moss
dripping tiny red chiggers, rehearsal for cobras and leeches.
Slog through that on your training tour
and you're ready for Charlie.
No, just ready to act brave.
And I, safe in new womanhood,
pretended to understand the choices:
Canada, conscientious objection, killing.

II. My Lai, 1998

Skinny gook girls planted the mines
they said, VC grannies tossed grenades
so what could we do but blow
the village into that shallow ditch
like a forced gasp of dope smoke?

The eyes of U.S. vets on TV are round
like mine. While they tell the truth at last,
I hug my daughter closer,
kiss her black hair,
my daughter first named

like so many Vietnamese girls
for the nightingale.

Where palm leaves are enough to build a house
what does it take to record a memory?
Columns of file cabinets, big as green tanks
papers in buff folders, hanging on metal frames?

Here is all it takes:
a word on another word and another.
Do this over and over as often
as it takes as long as it takes
because there are no shiny black walls
anywhere with lists of villagers
no roll for children charred by napalm
for girls turned from farmers to whores
by war and hard currency.

III.  Charleston, 2001

Helicopters' thip-thip-thip makes me cry.
Big black ones whack brochure-perfect salt air,
startle my daughter from her bucket and shovel,
her eyes widen, so black the pupils disappear.
I bend over her to shield her head with my mortal body.

She says, "Helicopters help people.
Take sick people to the doctor
and give them a hug
and they'll be all better."

Her dad dances with her on the beach at twilight.
A smile flies on her face like the flag.

*2000*

# GONE GONE

After "The Conversation"
                    by Romare Bearden


Let the young ones go—most got no sense
anyhow. Just look at that guitar girl—
her Irish granny still lives next door, pearl
pasty cheeks redden in the least little dab of sun.
Girl took off to play music so loud
she shook loose her brains, but her Granny's
still proud of her.   Most of us have had the pride
leaked out through the mill whistle's wail
at five every morning after trains
roaring through at two-oh-two. Worse
than having a new baby all the time.
My baby daughter grew up, got on the train
herself, and now I listen at the far train whistle
saying gone         gone
gone         gone
clear as the blue mountains,
clear as wind chimes
clear as track lines
where good can cross to bad.

*1996*

# The Light of the Red Cross Cookie Room

At the counter for cola and cookies
too many lights drew darkness down,
blinded me and knocked me right over.

Where were you? the nurse asked,
one of three bending over me.
They must know something

about how I hid behind the light.
They wrapped my head in a damp rag,
elevated my feet, trussed my arm

with a blood-pressure cuff,
covered me with two wool afghans
crocheted by the blind ladies.

The cola volunteer pulled up a chair.
He was from Nevada, a missionary,
whose name tag said "Elder."

His smooth face said he couldn't tell me
anything about deity. When he asked if I knew
his church, my mouth opened

but my thoughts and words hung apart
like odd socks on a clothesline.
The elder saw a sheep under those afghans

so he poured me another cup of RC Cola
and handed me a fist full of Oreos.
Beside the quiet rock of his listening

the cola and cookies became new blood.
I gave up my crown of rags, left the elder behind
with his own brand of light,
took up my suede pumps and walked.

*1993*

## Vietnam Reliquary

Notre Dame de Paris. 1964.

Stooped Parisiennes in black knelt to kiss
the glass, dead center, over a shred
of St. Joseph's fingernail.
The plum-robed bishop flicked the Sign of the Cross
evanescent as ash.
In the colony, shrapnel ripped the lieutenant's side.
In his hand, a sliver blood-black
as a Mekong River leech.

Aux Deux Magots. Today.

Look at him across the café table.
Through the glaze of pastis in his eyes,
around the corner of his stories,
see his buddy's arm, his sergeant's foot,
helicopters, body bags,
the Saigon virgin given to him for thanks.
Turn his hand over, kiss his palm
dark with the shadows of river valleys.

*1989*

# Original Publication

## Paul Allen

"One up by Clayton," *New England Review/Bread Loaf Quarterly*; included in
   *American Crawl* by Paul Allen (University of North Texas Press, 1997)
"Against Healing," *Southern Poetry Review*
"All I Want for Christmas is My Two Front Teeth," *Alabama Literary Review*
"The Book of the River" *Northwest Review*
"Ground Forces," *Windhover* (under the title "The Constituent Elements")

## Jan Bailey

"Bag of Promise," *Poetry East*; included in *Midnight in the Guest Room* by Jan Bailey,
   (Leapfrog Press, 2004)
"Cathedral Woods: giving thanks," *Paper Clothes* by Jan Bailey (Emrys Press, 1995)
"Encounter," Indiana Review; included in *Paper Clothes*
"Maggie on an Upswing," *Passages North*; included in *Midnight in the Guest Room*
 "With What Wild Hand," *Passages North* (winner of the Elinor Benedict Poetry Prize);
   included in *Midnight in the Guestroom*

## Cathy Smith Bowers

"Snow," *The Georgia Review*, 1994
"Mother Land," *America*, 1992
"Orchids," *The Georgia Review*, 1997
"Learning How to Pray," *The Atlantic Monthly*, 1997
"You Can't Drive the Same Truck Twice," *The Georgia Review*, 1993

## Jessica Bundschuh

"The Routine of a Letter Writer," *Quarterly West*
"The Tsar's Daughter in the Forensic Lab," *The Paris Review*
"Open Like a Vowel," *Point: South Carolina's Independent Newspaper*

## Stephen Corey

"The World's Largest Poet Visits Rural Idaho," *The Florida Review* (v. 6, 1977);
   included in *The Last Magician* by Stephen Corey (Water Mark Press, 1981)
"Quilts," *The Georgia Review* (v. XXXV, no.1, Spring 1981); included in
   *The Last Magician*

## Robert Cumming

"Storm Light," *Southern Poetry Review*, 1996
"Sleeping in the Abbey," *The Devil's Millhopper*, 1997

## Carol Ann Davis

"Ars Poetica inside an Evans Photograph," *Poetry*, August 2003
"In the Room," *The Gettysburg Review*, Autumn 2002
"As Elsewhere," *Black Warrior Review*, Spring/Summer 1999
"Giacometti Portrait in Four Parts," *DoubleTake*, Spring 2000

## Debra Daniel

"Hunting the Mine Hill," *Tar River*, Spring 2002
"Hymn of Invitation," (winner, Guy Owen Prize) *Southern Poetry Review*,
    Spring/Summer 2003
"The Olive Oyl Tapes," *Gargoyle 47*

## Curtis Derrick

"Sonnet," *Spectrum*, 1967 (Huntsville High School)
"Gusta," *Tinderbox Quarterly*
"Faith Nabors," *The Black Fly Review*

## Linda Annas Ferguson

"My Mother Doesn't Know Me," Poetry Society of South Carolina
    (Ellen Douglas Everett Carruthers Memorial Award)
"The Question," *Last Chance to Be Lost*
"Cotton Mill Hill," *It's Hard to Hate a Broken Thing*

## Starkey Flythe

"Sophia Loren," *Kennesaw Review* (Caring)
"St. Francis renounces his earthly father," *Oberon*
"Cher" and "Heaven," *Paying the Anesthesiologist* (Ninety-Six Press,
    Furman University)

## Angela Kelly

"Should Beckett Write the Essay of the Divorceé," *Asheville Poetry Review*, 2000
"After Too Much Wine," *Rosebud*, Winter 2000
"The Book the Devil's Chaplain Might Write," *Sad Little Breathings & Other Acts
    of Ventriloquism*, PublishingOnLine, 2001
"In the Kitchen," *North American Review,* March 2003
"fear comes like a whistle, a depot, the train itself," *Luna*, Spring 2004

# John Lane

"Waking in the Blue Ridge," *As the World Around Us Sleeps* by John Lane
  (Briarpatch Press, 1992)
"Returning Home, Saxon Mills," *As the World Around Us Sleeps*
"The Small Losses," *As the World Around Us Sleeps*
"Sweet Tea," *Against Information & Other Poems* by John Lane
  (New Native Press, 1995)
"My Dead Father on Vacation," *The Dead Father Poems* by John Lane
  (Horse & Buggy Press/Holocene Press, 1999)

# Susan Ludvigson

"The Child's Dream," *The Georgia Review*; included in *Northern Lights*
  by Susan Ludvigson (LSU Press, 1982) and *Sweet Confluence, New and
  Selected Poems* by Susan Ludvigson (LSU Press, 2000)
"Lasting" *The Georgia Review*; included in *The Beautiful Noon of No Shadow*
  by Susan Ludvigson (LSU Press, 1986) and *Sweet Confluence, New and
  Selected Poems* (LSU Press, 2000)
"Not Swans," *Shenandoah*; included in *Sweet Confluence, New and Selected Poems*
  (LSU Press, 2000).
"Bin Laden in South Carolina," *Gettysburg Review*; included in *Escaping the House of
  Certainty* by Susan Ludvigson (scheduled for publication by LSU Press in 2006)

# Terri McCord

"Retribution," *Chiron Review*; anthologized in *Quintet* (Ninety-Six Press, 2003)
"Dark Side," anthologized in *Quintet*
"Sighting," *Talking River Review*; anthologized in *Quintet*
"Huntress," *Yemassee*, anthologized in *Quintet*

# Ron Rash

"July 1949," *The Journal*; included in *Eureka Mill* (Benchmark Press and
  Hub City Writers Project, 2001)
"The Exchange," *Virginia Quarterly Review*
"Back-eyed Susans," *Hiram Review*

# Warren Slesinger

"Our Bedroom in the Fields," *The American Poetry Review*
"The Ring of Dancers," *The Sewanee Review*
"The Virtue of Loneliness," *The South Carolina Review*

# Kathleen Whitten

"Light of the Red Cross Cookie Room," *Journal of the American Medical Association*
  (JAMA)
"Vietnam Reliquary," *Graham House Review*

# Biographies

## About the editor

Kwame Senu Neville Dawes is a tireless editor, actor, poet, musician, playwright and critic. Since 1992 he has been teaching English at the University of South Carolina where he is the Distinguished Poet-in-Residence. He also serves as director of the South Carolina Poetry Initiative, a statewide organization that works with libraries, museums, schools, colleges and community organizations to promote and celebrate the reading, writing and performing of poetry across South Carolina. Born in Ghana in 1962, Dawes grew up in Jamaica where he attended Jamaica College and the University of the West Indies at Mona. He has published eight collections of poetry and was a winner of the Pushcart Prize for best American poetry in 2001. A recent collection, *Midland*, was awarded the Hollis Summers Poetry Prize by Ohio University Press (2001). He writes a regular column on poetry, "Poetically Speaking," in Columbia's *The State* newspaper.

## About the artist

Marcelo Novo, who lives and works in Columbia, was born in Buenos Aires, Argentina, in 1963, and studied painting under the direction of the Surrealist painter Roberto Aizemberg, developing Automatism as a means of creation. In 1992, he moved to the United States where he received a master's degree from the University of South Carolina and taught art at Benedict College from 1995 to 1998. His art has been exhibited in solo and group exhibitions in galleries and museums throughout the United States and abroad. In addition, his work is in public and corporate collections, including those of the South Carolina State Arts Collection, the Cultural Council of Richland & Lexington Counties in South Carolina and the White House Christmas Ornaments Collection.

*T*he Hub City Writers Project serves readers and writers by publishing works that foster a sense of place and by sponsoring events and programs. Our metaphor of organization purposely looks backward to the nineteenth century when Spartanburg was known as the "hub city," a place where railroads converged and departed. As we enter the twenty-first century, Spartanburg has become a literary hub of South Carolina with an active and nationally celebrated core group of poets, fiction writers, and essayists. We celebrate these writers— and the ones not yet discovered—as one of our community's greatest assets. William R. Ferris, former director of the Center for the Study of Southern Cultures, says of the emerging South, "Our culture is our greatest resource. We can shape an economic base…And it won't be an investment that will disappear."